T/L/C
TENDER LOVING CARE

2000
TIPS ON DOG CARE

T/L/C
TENDER LOVING CARE

2000
TIPS ON DOG CARE

TIPPY

RITA AND VAL REEL

Illustrations by Ann Downs
Verses by Ruth Merdian

RIVAL PUBLISHERS
Everett, Washington

LIBRARY OF CONGRESS
CATALOG CARD NO.:   81-90394

    Reel, Rita, & Val Reel
       TLC (2000 tips on dog care).

    Everett, WA: Rival Pub.
    240 p.
    8110   810716

ISBN 0-9607100-1-9

For Additional Copies of This Book

RIVAL PUBLISHERS
P.O. Box 5628
Everett, Washington 98206-5628

CONTENTS

CONTENTS (cont.)

APPENDIX

INTRODUCTION

Suggestions in this book have come
From many a reliable source...
From breeders, owners, and experts
All of whom I heartily endorse.
                                    TIPPY

With plenty TLC, veterinarian assistance, and luck, our first dog "Blackout" lived for fourteen years. As other dogs joined our family, more information was accumulated.

In order to increase our knowledge of dog care, we began a file on useful tips. We questioned veterinarians, contacted breeders, conversed with dog trainers, and compared notes with other pet owners.

After years of collecting this knowledge, we decided the material in our bulging files could be helpful to other dog owners. We sifted through our materials for the most pertinent tips. We spent three more years of intensive research, classified the material for ease in locating the information, and prepared this manuscript.

For a lighter vein, we added whimsical verse by Ruth Merdian who has delighted others for years with her talent. Ann Downs has used her artistic ability to capture a lovable "Tippy" in provocative situations that dog owners recognize so well.

We do wish to remind the readers of TLC that if the tips given are contradictory to their veterinarian's advice, they are by all means, to follow his suggestions. His personal relationships with your dog make him better able to deal with the individual problem.

Any owner of TLC will find this book an indispensable aid in caring for his dog from the time he is a fluffy puppy until he becomes that faithful and trusting senior citizen.

DANGERS

An imposing array
  Of poisons and sprays
Are dangerous to pets —
  Good business for vets.

ADVICE

• Present day pets are exposed to so many toxic chemicals that it is impossible to list them all. Even a combination of two or more seemingly harmless ingredients can spell DANGER.

• Keep cabinet doors, especially those in kitchen, bathroom, and workshop shut at ALL times.

• Before bringing the new puppy home, check the house and premises for potential dangers. It is amazing how inquisitive and fast a little puppy can be.

• Before using a product, read the label carefully and follow directions.

• Take time to list all the potentially dangerous products that are used in YOUR home. Make a chart of the products, antidotes, and first aid treatments. A few minutes now may save heartbreak later.

PRODUCT	ANTIDOTE	FIRST AID

• Old medication may be dangerous or ineffective. Do NOT use after one year or expiration date.

• BE CONSTANTLY ALERT FOR POTENTIAL DANGERS IN YOUR ENVIRONMENT!

MAN-MADE DANGERS

AEROSOLS

- Aerosol sprays for grooming, insects, cooking, first aid, cleaning, etc. can be extremely dangerous if not used correctly.

- Observe warnings on every product.

- Never leave an aerosol container where the temperature may reach 120°F. or it might explode.

- DO NOT THROW A USED CAN IN A FIRE.

- Never puncture an aerosol spray can.

- Some dogs, unfortunately, like to chew on tin cans. If the teeth puncture an aerosol container, it will explode in his face.

- Sprays should be used only in a well-ventilated room.

- Except for special products used for defense, NEVER spray a dog's face as some products may cause irreparable damage to his eyes.

ANTI-FREEZE

- Animals are attracted by the aroma and taste of anti-freeze and coolants. Two tablespoons of this man-made danger can kill a small dog — smaller quantities can cause severe kidney damage.

  *The taste of anti-freeze
  Is a tempting delight.
  What's left should be
  In a can, sealed tight.*

- SEE Poisons, page 63.

ASPHYXIA

- Asphyxiation is due to a deficiency of oxygen and an excess of carbon dioxide in the blood.

- Do not allow puppies and dogs to play with plastic bags. They may become entangled and suffocate.

- Old refrigerators, discarded boxes, wells, and tiny closets are all potential hazards.

- Objects that block the air passage may cause asphyxiation.

- It may be necessary to give artificial respiration. SEE Artificial Respiration, page 46.

AUTOMOBILES

- A piece of reflector tape on your pet's collar may help motorists avoid your dog at night.

- A car parked in the sun can be a death trap for your pet. If your car is parked in the sun, the temperature can go from 70° to 100° in just a few minutes. Check this out with a thermometer before leaving your pet in a potential oven.

- Do not allow your dog to sleep under a car.

- Train your dog not to chase cars.   SEE pages 141, 184.

BABY POWDER

- British breeders, particularly those of toy breeds, have been warned against the use of talcum powder. Most talcums contain boric acid which could possibly poison a small dog.

BONES

- Chicken, fish, and pork bones splinter easily and may lodge in throat or pierce intestines. Beef knuckle bones are much safer.

Bones... Bones... Bones...
  Of chicken, pork, or fish
Have no place
  In my doggy dish.

- SEE Swallowed Foreign Objects, page 60.

CARBON MONOXIDE POISONING

- This colorless, odorless gas is very poisonous and could be fatal to your dog.

- For yourself, as well as your dog, check to see that your car's exhaust system is working properly.

- Never transport your dog in the trunk of a car.

- Propane gas heaters or stoves in a camper or an unventilated tent are dangerous if not vented properly.

- In case of monoxide poisoning, remove the dog to fresh air immediately.

- Give artificial respiration if breathing has stopped.

CARDBOARD BOXES

- Do not keep small puppies in cardboard boxes which have been sprayed with pesticides or have contained sprayed fruit.

CHOKE (TRAINING) COLLARS

- Choke collars should NEVER be worn except during training sessions.

- A dog should NEVER be tied while wearing a choke collar. He may become entangled on an object and hang himself.

CHRISTMAS TREE ORNAMENTS

- Many Christmas tree ornaments are thin and shatter easily. Broken ornaments leave sharp shards and splinters that are extremely hazardous if swallowed.

The glittering balls
On Christmas trees
Don't digest too well
You'll have to agree.

- SEE Swallowed Foreign Objects, page 60.

CLEANING PRODUCTS AND SPRAYS

• Do not use sprays or cleaners which contain PHENOL or CARBOLIC ACID. These ingredients, if improperly used, can be absorbed through the skin and are highly toxic. They can result in liver, kidney damage, or non-specific anemia.

• The following cleaning products should be used with great care as they may be dangerous to your dog: ammonia, drain cleaner, bleach, inflammable cleaning fluid, lye, oven cleaner, washing soda, furniture and floor waxes, and some toilet bowl cleaners.

• Sprays, such as deodorizers or those used on furniture, may also be harmful to pets.

• CALL YOUR VETERINARIAN.

COPPER

• High levels of copper in tap water can cause health and mental problems in pets. If you have copper pipes in your home, let the water run for 30 to 60 seconds to clear the pipes before using.

DRAIN CLEANERS

• Grease dissolvers for sluggish drains generally kept in cabinets in the kitchen or bathroom are extremely hazardous to your pet. Swallowing even a small amount may cause permanent damage to the esophagus. KEEP CABINET DOORS CLOSED.

DROWNING

• If an unattended dog falls into a swimming pool, he could drown if no provision, such as a ramp, is provided for his escape.

DYED MATS

- Some dogs, like some people, are allergic to dye. A dyed mat laid on the floor of a sleeping basket may, in some dogs, cause skin irritation or other problems.

ELECTRIC SHOCK — PREVENTION

- The shock of 110 volts could kill a dog.

- Tabasco Sauce or Bitter Apple applied to electric cords may be a deterrent to cord-chewing puppies.

- The only safe solution is to unplug all electrical devices. Puppies are especially attracted to the soft, chewable cords.

- SEE Electric Shock, page 56.

FIRE

- Fires often occur when occupants are not at home. Your pet may become a victim if firemen are unaware of the presence of your dog. This is especially true if he is crated.

- Write to Friends of Animals, Inc., Dept. 516, 11 West 60th Street, New York, N.Y. 10023 for a decal to place in a window alerting the fire fighters of the presence and approximate area pet may be found.

FLEA COLLARS AND DIPS

- Do not use a flea collar on a dog that has received medication for worms.

- Flea collars are helpful in most cases. However, some dogs may be allergic to the chemicals in flea collars and develop skin irritation or bronchial problems.

- Do not use an insecticidal dip on your dog before putting on a flea collar. Use one or the other — not both.

- Flea dips are potentially dangerous to your dog if directions are not carefully followed.

- Do not store unused mixed flea dip. If the water evaporates, the concentration of chemicals could burn the dog.

- Be sure the veterinarian is aware that your dog is, or has recently worn a flea collar. Some dogs have less tolerance for certain medication or even normal dosages of anesthesia if they have been exposed to the chemicals in a flea collar.

GARAGES

- A dog housed in a garage is exposed to innumerable dangers. Keep aerosols, petroleum products, solvents, cleaners, corrosive and rust inhibitors, antifreeze, coolants, lubricants, etc., etc., etc., in a locked cabinet.

- If you change the coolant and antifreeze, make sure the pans, funnels and any spills on the floor are cleaned up. The old used portions should be disposed of in a safe manner. Two tablespoons can be fatal to a small dog.

- Do not warm up your car with the garage door closed.

GOLF BALLS

- Golf balls may explode when pierced as they are formed under high pressure. They also contain sulfuric acid, zinc sulfide, lead oxide, etc. They are not safe toys.

There's bad stuff inside
That old golf ball.
Pieces could lodge
In my stomach wall.

HAY OR STRAW DUST

- The dust from hay or straw sometimes used for bedding is capable of setting up an allergic reaction affecting the bronchi and lungs. It may cause pneumonia.

HERBICIDES

- Before spraying a garden to control undesirable plants, read the directions carefully. Many chemicals are highly toxic.

- If plant life looks brown and withered, it may indicate the area was sprayed for weed control. Do not allow your dog to run in a field which has been treated with herbicides.

- Your dog probably will not eat the sprayed plant, but the poison can be absorbed through the skin and lungs.

HOUSE PLANTS

- Do not keep poisonous plants in the house. Even if the plant is out of reach, a leaf or bloom that has fallen to the floor can be dangerous.

- Call the Poison Control Center for antidote.

- SEE Poisons, page 63.

HUMAN MEDICINE

- Avoid doctoring your dog with your own prescriptions. Tolerance and overdosage are common dangers. Consult your veterinarian.

- A safety cap may be child proof but dogs and puppies can crush the plastic bottles.

- If your dog has ingested pills, immediately call your veterinarian, Poison Control Center, or pharmacist.

INHALATION

- If a room has been fumigated, do not allow pets to enter until it has been thoroughly aired.

- Do not permit your dog in a room where there is the danger of inhaling strong fumes from airplane glue, cleaning fluids, gas leaks, paint, lacquer, or smoke.

- Death may result when oil-based medication enters the windpipe and lungs through inhalation. The safest method of administration is to form a pocket in the bottom lip, pour in small amounts of medication and rub the throat to encourage swallowing.

LAWN MOWERS

- Keep pets away from area that is being mowed. Dogs have lost eyes from flying rocks. Feet have been amputated by the whirling blades.

LEAD POISONING

- Lead poisoning affects liver, kidneys, and brain. Prompt medical attention is needed. Symptoms are abdominal pains and convulsions.

Too many playthings
May contain lead.
Too much of that
And I could be dead.

- Since the early 1970's, lead has not been used in residential paints. However, some older homes have been painted with lead-based paints. This is dangerous if your pet chews on the painted surface. Some commercial paints still contain lead.

- Lead compounds, commonly used in ceramic glazes, are harmless if they are properly applied and fired; if unfired, they are potentially dangerous.

- Colored magazines and newspapers contain enough lead to poison a child or a dog.

- Paint flakes from old toys can be chewed off and cause lead poisoning. Present-day paints, however, do not contain lead.

- Linoleum, roofing supplies, lead fishing sinkers, golf balls, etc. are only a few of the hazardous products containing lead that are found in our environment.

PLASTICS

- The convenience of plastics has added another hazard to the dogs' world. Plastic is completely indigestible and may cause life-threatening blockage.

- If the dog becomes entangled in plastics (laundry bags, etc.) there is the danger of asphyxiation.

- Plastics can cause severe allergic reactions in some dogs.

RAT POISON

- Numerous poisons are used to exterminate rodent pests. Inform your veterinarian of the type used. Many are odorless and tasteless. Phosphorus leaves a garlic-like odor on the breath.

- Immediately call the veterinarian or Poison Control Center.

- If a dog has eaten rat poison which contains phosphorus, do not feed him eggs, oil, fats, or milk for several days after he is on the road to recovery.

- SEE Poisons, page 63.

REDWOOD CHIPS

- Commercial chips used for landscaping are extremely dangerous as they have been chemically treated to protect them from mildew and rot.

ROCK SALT

- Rock salt and commercial chemicals used to melt ice on sidewalks and roads are quite harmful to your pet. Besides burning the pads, the ingestion of the chemicals and salt by licking may result in poisoning or dehydration. Wash dog's feet with a mild soap after walking through the snow or ice.

Salt does the job
Of melting your ice.
What it does to my feet
Isn't all that nice.

SAWDUST

- Although sawdust is suitable bedding for large breeds of dogs, it should never be used for the Chihuahua or other tiny dogs or puppies of any breed. It can become most dangerous when it gets into the eyes or is mixed into food.

- If a puppy eats sawdust, it can cause intestinal blockage. This must be eliminated, either naturally or by surgery.

SCALDING

- A large dog, standing on his hind legs, can scald himself by knocking pans off the stove. Turn pot handles away so he can't reach them or train him to stay away from the stove.

- SEE Burns, page 49.

SLUG AND SNAIL BAIT

- These products contain deadly poisons. They have a sweetish taste which is as attractive to the puppy as it is to the pest.

- Emergency care is a must! Call the veterinarian immediately.

SPRAYS, HAIR

- Women shouldn't use hair spray when the family dog is near, warned a veterinary surgeon at a meeting of the British Small Animal Veterinary Association. Dogs are often allergic to hair spray and can develop a form of asthma from careless exposure to the fumes.

Various cans
Containing sprays
Can cause us pets
Some miserable days.

TOILET BOWL CLEANERS

- Some dogs will drink out of a toilet bowl! If you have such an animal, NEVER use toilet bowl cleaners that hang inside of the tank unless you check label to see whether it is safe for your pet.

- If in the process of using a chemical to clean the toilet bowl you are called away, be sure to put the lid down in your absence.

- After cleaning with a chemical, flush the toilet at least twice.

TOOTHPICKS

- A toothpick can be lethal. Its pointed ends may pierce the intestines. Prevention is better than the cure.

- SEE Foreign Objects, page 60.

TOYS

- Toys and balls that are too small may be swallowed.

- Soft rubber toys may be chewed up and the pieces, when swallowed, may cause blockage.

- Dogs may tear open a squeaky toy and swallow the metal noisemaker.

- Soft, washable animal toys may be chewed and the cotton or foam stuffing swallowed causing serious blockage.

- A large breed, adult dog, may swallow a cotton sock or nylon panty hose which has been given to him as a toy.

- SEE Foreign Objects, page 60.

TV DINNER TRAYS

- Don't feed dogs out of disposable aluminum trays. A dog may chew on it and swallow pieces. The sharp edges can cut and puncture the intestinal wall.

- SEE Foreign Objects, page 60.

NATURE'S DANGERS

There's a list
As long as your arm...
Of hazardous plants
That do me harm.

FLOWERS, TREES, VEGETABLES, ETC.

- You may be aware of the poisonous plants in your area; but if you move to another section of the country, you will find dangerous plants indigenous to that region only. Check with your public library or agricultural department.

- **Flower Garden Plant** — **Toxic Part**

Flower Garden Plant	Toxic Part
Autumn Crocus	All parts
Azalea	All parts
Bleeding Heart	All parts
Buttercup	All parts
Daphne	All parts
Delphinium	All parts
Foxglove	Leaves, seed
Hyacinth	Bulb
Hydrangea	All parts
Iris	Leaves, roots
Jessamine	Flowers, berries
Larkspur	All parts
Laurel	All parts
Lily-of-the-valley	All parts
Monkshood	All parts
Narcissus	Bulb
Peony	Roots
Tulip	Bulb

- **House Plants**

Castor bean	Entire plant
Christmas rose	All parts

- **House Plants** (cont.)

Chrysanthemum	Resin from the stems
Dieffenbachia	All parts
Elephant ear	All parts
Holly	Berries
Ivy	Leaves
Mistletoe	Entire plant
Philodendron	All parts
Poinsettia	All parts
Rosary pea	All parts

- **Ornamental Plants**

Boxwood	All parts
Daffodil	Bulb
English Ivy	Berries, leaves
Golden Chain	Seeds, pods, flowers
Mountain Laurel	All parts
Oleander	All parts
Wisteria	Pods, seeds

- **Trees**

Apple	Seeds, large quantities
Apricot	Pits
Avocado	Leaves, stems, pods
Black Locust	Bark, seeds, and leaves
Cherry	Stones
English Holly	Berries
Horse Chestnut	All parts
Oak	Leaves, acorns
Oleander, yellow	All parts
Peaches	Stones
Yew	All parts

- **Vegetables**

Eggplant	Foliage, sprouts
Potato	All parts except tuber
Rhubarb	Leaves
Tomato	Leaves

EXERCISE

I love to flex my muscles;
  It keeps me fit and trim.
Exercise should be regular
  Not at someone's whim.

AMOUNT

- Dogs have been bred for different purposes so some breeds need more exercise than others. Dogs in the Working Group require more physical activity than those in the Toy Group.

- All house dogs should be walked regularly three times a day to answer Nature's call and to receive the benefit of fresh air and sunshine.

- Even small dogs need some outdoor activity.

- Large dogs need, in addition to the three walks around the block, at least a half hour of active play or exercise.

- Older dogs, ten years or more, should be exercised regularly, but the amount curtailed.

- An isolated dog, in an enclosed area, does not have the incentive for much exercise. Add another dog as a companion and they will run, chase, tease, and play throughout the day.

- Dogs in the city should not be allowed to run free in order to get their exercise because you haven't the time or inclination to walk them on a leash. It would be far better if you would get a cat, bird, or goldfish for a pet.

- Check with your veterinarian as to the physical condition of your dog and as to the amount of exercise your dog requires. A dog with a history of heart problems should not be exercised vigorously.

AUTOMATIC EXERCISER

- This machine, although expensive, helps to condition your dog without any effort on your part. Check ads in dog magazines or get additional information from pet supply stores.

- Hook dog to machine and turn on. Speed can be varied.

- The workouts should be short when first starting.

- Give treat to dog after each session so that he will look forward to his time on the exerciser.

BALL RETRIEVING

- Start your puppy early to retrieve a thrown ball.

- This is a natural activity for sporting dogs, other breeds may have to be taught.

- This activity provides plenty of exercise for the dog, and you will not need to take long walks with your pet in inclement weather.

BENEFITS

- A physically fit dog is better able to withstand disease.

- Exercise maintains mental alertness.

- Physical activity slows down the aging process.

- Exercise helps to firm up muscles and prevent obesity.

BICYCLING

- This type of exercise may be dangerous to the bicyclist, pedestrian, or motorist if the dog is not well trained.

- Young puppies should not be exercised in this manner.

- Do not use this form of exercise if there is traffic.

- Do not fasten leash to the bicycle — hold it in your hand.

- Take short trips at first until the dog's pads harden and he builds up endurance.

BIG DOGS — LITTLE YARD

- One ingenious man solved the exercise problem of his big dogs in a little yard by building a FENCED-IN platform around a tree with a FENCED-IN ramp to the platform. The dogs happily scurried up and down all day checking out the neighborhood.

CHILDREN

- Dogs lucky enough to live in a family with children generally get sufficient exercise. If there are no children in the family, invite some neighborhood youngsters to romp with your dogs.

CLEAN-UP EQUIPMENT

- When exercising your dog in a city, carry a household plastic bag. Fit the bag over your hand and pick up your dog's waste. Turn bag inside out, tie, and put in nearest disposal can.

- Aluminum, plastic, or styrofoam trays such as used for rolls, meats, etc., cut in half, make excellent throw-away scoopers. Put stools and scooper in plastic bag and discard.

- A true story: A lady walking her dog always picked up the stools and put them in an old purse to dispose of later at home. A purse-snatcher grabbed it!

COLD-WEATHER EXERCISE

- House dogs are sensitive to the elements. In walking a small, short-haired dog or an old dog in cold or wet weather, it is wise to slip a sweater on him.

DAILY EXERCISE

- Dogs MUST have exercise. If your schedule doesn't permit time for you to exercise your dog, hire a responsible child or senior citizen to walk your dog daily.

Walking 'round the block
For me will be O.K.
Please remember I need it
Several times a day.

DEFENSE

- In walking your dog on a leash, you might experience the unpleasant situation of an unleashed dog threatening yours. Stand your ground and try one of the following:

  - Load a water pistol with a solution of one teaspoon ammonia to one pint of water.

  - The liquid from an artificial lemon squirted in the dog's face is a deterrent.

  - Arm yourself with a "gun" containing a chemical, non-hazardous solvent that will incapacitate the offender. It sends a stream six to ten feet. Postmen and meter readers often use such devices. Call your law enforcement agencies for information as this device is illegal in some areas.

  - Carry an electric stock prod. It is powered by batteries and gives a shock to the attacking animal. May be purchased at feed or farm supply stores.

DOG SOCCER

- If dogs are penned up and show no inclination to exercise, put several old soccer balls in their area. They will enjoy pushing them around.

DOG TENDER REEL

- Consists of a steel stake, a reel, and a 15-foot cable which extends and retracts automatically. This allows 700 square feet of exercise area.

DOG TROLLIES

- The safest way to keep a dog tied is to stretch heavy gauge steel wire taut between two posts with the wire about six feet above the ground. A steel chain snapped around the wire and fastened to the dog's collar allows him a longer exercise area. The chain should be short enough so he will not become tangled yet long enough to permit him to lie down.

- Instead of an overhead trolly, drive two stakes in the ground. Slide a ring on a wire and fasten ends tightly between the two stakes. Connect the rope or leash to the ring. This device allows dog greater area to exercise without tangling. CAUTION: Place in an area where people will not trip over it.

DOGGY DIP

- Exercising your dog in public areas exposes him to numerous germs and diseases. On returning home, dip your dog's feet in a mixture of 30:1 of water and Clorox. Pour the mixture in a shallow pan covered with a lid or screen. The pan and an old towel, placed at the entrance, simplifies this safeguard.

FRISBEE

- Catching a Frisbee is excellent exercise. Provides variety.

IRREGULARITY

- For a dog to be without exercise for days and then taken out for a few hours or even minutes of vigorous running can be injurious. It can cause strain and tension in muscles weakened by disuse. Irregular exercise can bring on medical and emotional problems. It can also speed up the aging process, or aggravate a chronic medical problem.

JOGGING

- Jogging is great exercise for you and your pet.

- Do NOT jog with a very young puppy.

- Keep your dog on a leash unless he is well trained.

- Too much exertion at first is not good for your dog.

KENNEL DOGS

- Kennel dogs need frequent human companionship. In your fenced-in yard, romp and play with your kennel dog for, at least, 15 to 30 minutes every day.

MERRY-GO-ROUND

- If your dog needs exercise and you don't, tie a long cord to a pole. At the end of the cord, tie an old sock filled with tidbits. Allow the dog to smell it, then swing in a wide circle. The dog will attempt to catch it. At the end of the exercise, reward him with the goodies.

OBEDIENCE TRAINING

- Great exercise for you and your dog is to participate in an obedience class. An extra bonus is the opportunity to socialize with other dogs and people.

- Practicing each day for proficiency will provide additional exercise which is so beneficial to both of you.

- Obedience classes include training your dog to heel, run, jump, retrieve, and obey simple commands.

- Field and Tracking classes provide additional exercise in the fresh air.

OBSTACLE COURSE

- Set up jumps which the dog can clear with ease. Lay several boards down for a broad jump. Find a big drain tile or carton he has to crawl through. Set up a narrow board off the ground for him to "tight-walk" on. Provide a ramp he can climb. Use your imagination and materials at hand. Reward him generously at the completion of the course.

PAVED SURFACES

- Whatever you do, don't exercise your dog on paved surfaces regularly or for long distances. Owners of race horses know that this breaks the pasterns down and the same may be true of dogs — especially puppies.

SOCCER

- This activity is fun for the larger dog and provides a great deal of exercise. Two or more people kick a soccer ball around allowing the dog to get possession of it once in awhile. However, if you ever wish to have a serious game, the dog could be a real nuisance for he certainly delights in this sport.

SWIMMING

- Swimming comes naturally to dogs in the sporting group, others may have to be encouraged.

- Throw a stick or ball in the water for him to retrieve.

- Be careful of overexertion.

- Unless the weather is warm, dry your dog carefully after he has played in the water.

- If swimming in a pool, be sure there is a graded exit where your dog can get out by himself; otherwise, he will tire, become frightened, or even drown.

TAILGATING

- This exercise is rather strenuous so check with your veterinarian as to your dog's physical condition.

- For large dogs that need a great deal of exercise, tailgating is excellent but can be dangerous if care is not taken.

  - Prevent the dog from running under the car by attaching the lead to a pole and hold horizontally while sitting on the open tailgate of a station wagon.

  - Use untraveled roads.

  - Regulate the speed to the dog's ability.

  - Check the pads frequently.

  - Start out slowly and for short distances.

TRACKING

- This is a game of hide-and-seek. Begin by letting your dog see you place a goodie then tell him to find it. Eventually, you could substitute other things and make it harder for him by going out of sight and backtracking before you hide the article. Dogs have a keen sense of smell and will be guided by the scent of your footsteps. Excellent training for tracking.

TUG-OF-WAR

- This game is fun between two dogs or owner and dog but is very bad for a puppy's teeth — an otherwise good bite could be ruined. For some dogs, it can develop aggressive characteristics. For an adult, timid dog, this exercise could be good.

- Use blue jeans, or any sturdy material for this game.

FEEDING

I have my owner trained
To feed me what I wish,
Or I look at him reproachfully
And leave it in my dish.

ADDITIVES

- In adding meat scraps, broth, etc. to commercial dog food, do not exceed 25 percent of the total rations.

AMOUNT

- Many factors must be considered in the amount to feed your dog, such as, age, obesity, activity, etc.

- Over-feeding is more harmful than under-feeding.

- If your veterinarian says your dog is at an ideal weight, feed only the amount that maintains that weight.

APPETITE

- If a dog refuses to eat a meal or two, don't worry. After he refuses food for two days, consult a veterinarian.

- Should your dog appear eager to eat but leaves the food, check his mouth for a bad tooth, something foreign in his mouth, or a sore throat.

AUTOMATIC FEEDER

- An automatic feeder keeps the food dry and is always accessible to the dog. Food bills can be cut by using self-feeding as the dog eats only what he needs.

- BE SURE WATER IS ALWAYS AVAILABLE.

BALANCE

- An overabundance of meat, vegetables, or roughage may result in indigestion, vomiting, skin irritation, bloat, gas, or constipation. Balance is the key to good nutrition.

CANINE COOKIES

- Homemade cookies are nutritious, inexpensive, and fun to make.

- The three recipes given are basic. Use your imagination to create other treats.

- Reduce or increase the amounts depending on number and size of the dogs.

- There are no preservatives used to maintain freshness. Bake several batches at one time and store in the freezer.

- Avoid bleached white flour as much as possible. Use whole wheat, rye, bran, rolled oats, or corn meal.

- The crunchier and drier the cookie the better it is for the dog's teeth. This may be accomplished by turning off the heat and leaving the cookies in the oven for an extra ten minutes.

- **TIPPY'S TREATS**

      2   eggs beaten
      3   tablespoons blackstrap molasses
      ¼   cup vegetable oil
      ¼   cup milk
      1   cup rolled oats
      ¾   cup wheat germ
      ¼   cup white flour
      ½   cup raisins (optional)

    Mix ingredients and drop by teaspoon on a lightly greased baking sheet. Bake at 350° for 15 minutes. Turn off the temperature and allow TIPPY'S TREATS to dry until they are crunchy.

- **BACON BITS**

  6   slices of fried bacon, crumbled
  4   eggs beaten
  ⅛   cup bacon drippings plus vegetable oil
  1   cup water
  ½   cup powdered non-fat milk
  2   cups graham flour
  2   cups wheat germ
  ½   cup corn meal

  Follow directions for TIPPY'S TREATS. Cook at 350° for 25 minutes.

- **GARLIC GOODIES**

  2   eggs beaten
  ¼   cup honey
  2   cups water
  ½   cup of oil
  1   cup of powdered milk
  1   cup of white flour
  4   cups graham flour
  2   tbls. garlic powder

  Dozens of dog biscuits
  On your grocer's shelf,
  But I'm fond of those
  You make yourself.

  Mix and roll out ½ inch thick. Cut with bone- or dog-shaped cookie cutter. Strips, squares, or circles may also be used. Sprinkle with garlic powder and place on lightly greased baking sheet. Bake 350° for 20 minutes.

CHANGING DIETS

- A sudden change in a dog's diet may cause a digestive upset. To accomplish the changeover, add a small amount of the new food gradually until the new diet is established.

CHICKEN

- In its protein content, poultry is equal or superior to the finest red meat.

- Chicken is excellent for dogs with a kidney problem.

- Cook chicken in a pressure cooker until bones are completely dissolved. It will form a jelly when cool. Pour over dry food for added flavor and nutrition.

- Chicken soup is excellent for sick or recuperating dogs.

COMMERCIAL DOG FOOD

- **Canned Dog Food**

  - The sole use of canned food encourages tartar to form on the teeth. For that reason, it might be a good idea to mix the moist food with some dry food.

  - Canned (moist) food should contain at least 3/10 percent calcium.

  - Do not buy canned (moist) food that contains more than 75 percent water.

  - Visually examine the contents of several cans. If foreign objects are observed, switch to another brand.

- **Dry Dog Food**

  - Dry food acts as an abrasive on teeth and helps keep them clean.

  - Avoid torn or resealed bags.

  - Food should not be stored for long periods of time so avoid dealers where the turnover is low.

  - Never use galvanized containers to store food as they contain toxic zinc.

  - To avoid an infestation of insects and rodents, store food in containers with tight-fitted lids.

- When dry food is served, make sure plenty of fresh water is available.

- **Label Information**

  - Attractive packaging and expensive advertising does not guarantee adequate or proper nourishment for your dog. Read the labels carefully. Better still, write to the company for a complete analysis of the food. Compare with other brands and discuss with your veterinarian.

    If you're planning my dinner,
    This is what I wish...
    Read the labels carefully
    Before you fill my dish.

  - If you are feeding your dog a brand that is nutritionally complete, you must feed what is recommended for your size dog; otherwise, he will not receive sufficient nutrition, vitamins, or minerals.

  - Main ingredients are listed first. Be sure that in moist foods, animal protein is listed in the first two ingredients; in dry food, the first three ingredients.

DIGESTION

- Put a meat tenderizer in the dog's food to help digestion.

- To prevent stomach upset, avoid spiced, fried, or greasy foods.

- Buttermilk helps restore normal healthy bacteria to the intestinal tract.

DIGESTIVE TIME

- It takes an average of sixteen hours for food to pass through the dog's digestive system.

DISHES

- Some pottery and earthenware contain dangerous amounts of lead which is hazardous to animals unless properly fired.

- Probably the best and least expensive dish is the stainless steel bowl. It is practically indestructible and can be sterilized.

- A dish is now manufactured for the long-eared dog. This prevents wet and dirty ears. Available at pet supply stores.

- For large dogs, raise food dishes off the floor. It is more comfortable and helps to avoid neck and back problems. Use an old wooden box or child's play table about one to two feet high. Cut holes to fit the food and water dishes.

FATTY ACIDS

- Diets may be supplemented with vegetable oil or bacon fat — one teaspoon to one pound of dry food.

- Check the label of canned dog food. If it contains more than six percent fat, do not add additional fat.

- If fat content is more than 40 percent of the daily caloric requirement, it could cause nutritional deficiency.

- Lack of fat in the diet can cause the hair to be coarse and the skin to be dry.

FISH

- Even a tiny bit of raw salmon or trout CAN KILL. It may be a host to a virus-transmitting fluke. The symptoms are refusal to eat, depression, and extreme thirst. Unfortunately, these symptoms do not appear for ten to fourteen days after the salmon is eaten.

GULPING FOOD

- Divide the daily allotment of food into several small meals.

- If a dog gulps his food, try using a larger pan. In this pan, put two or three LARGE STONES. This will slow the eating process. Be sure to keep the stones, as well as the dishes, clean.

INEXPENSIVE DOG BISCUITS

- Many bakery outlets sell day-old bread at a discount. Whole wheat or rye bread is very nutritious. Do not use white bread. Cube the bread and dry it out in the oven at 200° for two hours. Sprinkle with garlic powder to make it tastier.

- From a bakery, purchase day-old bagels. Allow them to dry until quite hard. Dogs think this is a great treat, and it also helps to reduce tartar on the teeth.

LEFTOVERS

- **Tips for Saving**

  - Instead of putting potato peelings, carrot scrapings, celery tops, etc. into the garbage can, make a tasty doggy stew. Add several cups of water and cook, at least, 15 minutes.

  - If a loaf of bread has become dry or moldy, don't throw it out. It is a real treat for the dogs and high in calories for those who need a little extra weight. Could also be added to homemade stews.

  - If dog leaves portions of his meal, put the leftovers in a plastic bag and place in the refrigerator until the next meal. Discard after the second attempt. Never allow moist food to remain in the dish all day at room temperature.

  - Butcher shops and meat packers often have scraps and organ meats which they sell at lower prices.

MILK

- Milk is an excellent food source of calcium and vitamins. Unfortunately, it causes problems, such as diarrhea, in some dogs. Because of its food values, before eliminating milk entirely from the dog's diet, try reducing the amount given.

- Buttermilk is excellent for a "gassy" dog. Give one cup daily for large dogs.

- If a dog's digestion is upset or the dog has been on a heavy dosage of antibiotics, give one tablespoon of buttermilk every day to get digestion back to normal.

- Goat's milk is excellent for sickly and underweight puppies and dogs.

ORGAN FOOD

- Liver, kidney, lungs, brains, tripe, and sweetbread, are very nutritious and provide necessary vitamins and minerals. The broth is a tasty treat over dry food.

- When cooking organ foods, add tomato juice to disguise the aroma.

- **Special Treat.** Boil liver in salted water with several cloves of garlic. Remove and cut in bite size. Place on a cookie sheet and bake at 250° for several hours. The broth can be poured over dry dog food for added nutrition and taste.

- Liver is very nutritious and dogs love it. It can, however, cause diarrhea in some animals but is great for dogs that have a tendency toward constipation.

- Boil any organ meat for a short time then remove from the water and cut in bite size. Return to the kettle and add vegetables (25 percent) and cereal (25 percent). Cook until done.

OVERWEIGHT DOGS

- Check Special Diets for obesity.

- Reduce the amount of food but add vitamins and minerals.

- Provide more exercise. Keep physical condition of dog in mind.

PICKY EATERS

- **Tips to Tempt**

  - Liver or chicken cat food usually tempts the pickiest eater.

  - In summer, when appetites may lag, add salt to the food. Onion powder also gets results.

  - Brewer's yeast works wonders with the erratic or picky eater. Give one teaspoon to 25 pounds of dog's weight, daily.

  - Bits of luncheon meat, hidden under the regular food, often tempts the fussy eater.

  - Food mixed with hot water brings out the flavor of food.

  - A jaded appetite can be tempted with fish (cat food or tuna).

  - Cheese is very nutritious and tempting to the picky eater; however, it may be constipating.

  - Butter or margarine rubbed along the rim of the dish often primes the fussy eater.

SPECIAL DIETS

- **Bland Diets**

  - Cook rice, grits, or noodles and add to chicken or beef broth.

  - Serve boiled egg with buttered toast.

- Cook cereal such as Wheatina, Farina, etc.

- Baby foods offer a wide range of bland foods.

- **Cold Weather Diets**

  - Increase amounts of food which are high in calories and fat to produce energy and body heat. Do not increase carbohydrate foods such as vegetables which are low in fat.

- **Hot Weather Diets**

  - Reduce the quantity of food.

  - Serve a little less fat.

  - Feed very early in the morning or late at night.

- **Obesity Diet**

  - Overfeeding is not always the cause of obesity. Check with your veterinarian on the many possibilities before subjecting your dog to a weight-reduction program.

  - Prescription diets for overweight dogs may be purchased from your veterinarian.

  - The change in diet should be gradual.

  - Keep a daily record (for a week) of kinds and amounts of food given to your dog before discussing this problem with your veterinarian.

  - Homemade obesity diets may be made with lean meat, green beans, carrots, and cottage cheese. These ingredients provide bulk but have fewer calories.

- Divide the daily rations into several small meals. Your dog will not be so indignant at the reduced allowance.

- **Prescription Diets**

  - There are canned prescription diets for heart, kidney, or intestinal disease which may be obtained from your veterinarian. There are special diets for obesity and puppies.

  - These canned prescription diets are identified in the following ways:

        HD   Heart trouble
        KD   Older dogs with kidney trouble
        LD   Bland diet
        PD   Puppy diet
        RD   Low calories for overweight.

- **Stress Diet**

  - Provide an animal under stress with good quality protein, moderate amount of fat, and good quality carbohydrates.

  - Protein sources are boiled eggs, meat, and cottage cheese. Carbohydrates are found in cooked cereals, rice, and oatmeal. Use vegetable oils for fat.

- **Underweight Diet**

  - For a weight gain in small dogs, add 1 teaspoon of peanut oil and ½ teaspoon of honey to food.

  - Brewer's yeast (one teaspoon to 25 pounds of dog's weight) will increase the appetite and help to put on weight.

  - Sprinkle malted milk over the food.

- Try a different brand, add canned food to the dry, make a doggy stew, or add tasty broths to the food.

- Add raisins to the dog food. One-half cup of raisins provides 225 calories.

- Mix instant potato flakes into the food.

- Goats' milk is excellent for underweight dogs and puppies.

STEWS

- Meat should constitute at least 40 to 50 percent of the stew mixture. Add vegetables and brown rice. Be sure the rice is thoroughly cooked — at least, one half hour.

- Ingredients for homemade dog food must include water, protein, carbohydrates, fats, vitamins and minerals to meet the MDR (Minimum Daily Requirements).

- Depending on the ingredients used, homemade dog food may not contain sufficient vitamins and minerals for MDR and supplementation is needed. However, indiscriminate additions are dangerous, especially vitamins A and D. Discuss this with your veterinarian.

STOOLS

- A dog's stools may be an indication of improper feeding if any of the following problems are present:

  1. Diarrhea

  2. Flatulence

  3. Excessive amount (too much cereal or indigestible material)

TIDBITS

- Never feed your dog at the table or give tidbits during the day. Delicious table scraps tend to make your dog a picky eater.

- Irregular feeding of tidbits results in an unbalanced diet.

TIME AND PLACE

- Dogs are creatures of habit and will be happier if they are fed at the same time and place. They do not like eating side by side, so place dishes apart or on opposite sides of the room.

VITAMINS AND MINERALS

- Vitamins and mineral supplements are needed if your dog is not eating the amount of food recommended on commercial dog food labels. This is especially true for the obese dog whose daily allotment has been reduced.

Vitamins galore
From A to Z...
A whole bottle
Is not for me.

- Over supplementation of certain vitamins may be harmful. Consult your veterinarian.

WARNINGS

- Do not feed your dog several hours before strenuous exercise.

- After vigorous exercise, allow the dog to rest for, at least, a half hour before feeding.

- To prevent gastro-intestinal problems, including bloat, it might be better to serve several small feedings a day instead of one big meal.

WATER CONSUMPTION

- Change your dog's drinking water, at least, once a day — more often in hot weather.

TIPPY PRICKS FOOD FALLACIES

1. SWEETS ARE HARMFUL
2. DIFFERENT BREEDS EAT DIFFERENT FOODS
3. DOGS CAN'T EAT STARCH
4. MOIST FOOD CAUSES TARTAR
5. RAW EGGS MAKE SHINY COATS
6. PORK IS HARMFUL
7. RAW MEAT MAKES DOGS VICIOUS
8. MILK CAUSES WORMS
9. DOGS SHOULDN'T HAVE MILK
10. ALL MEAT DIET IS BEST

1. Only in excess.
2. A dog is a dog.
3. No harm if it is cooked.
4. All foods produce tartar.
5. Raw egg whites destroy biotin.
6. Not if well cooked.
7. Myth began when dog defended his food.
8. Not true.
9. Milk is nutritious but may cause diarrhea.
10. Dogs need nutrients not found in meat alone.

FIRST AID

Let's check the medicine cabinet
To find what I will need
When I'm injured, ill,
Or just plain off my feed.

FIRST AID IS THE IM-MEDIATE AND TEM-PORARY CARE GIVEN YOUR PET UNTIL PROFESSIONAL HELP IS AVAILABLE.

FIRST AID SUPPLIES

Activated Charcoal	Boric Acid	Spirits of Ammonia
Adhesive Tape	Eye Ointment	Sterile Cotton
Antihistamine	Gauze Bandaging	Teaspoon
Antiseptic Powder	Hydrogen Peroxide	Thermometer
Baking Soda	Kaopectate	Tweezers
Blunt Scissors	Milk of Magnesia	Vaseline

VITAL SIGNS

- Check vital signs (pulse, respiration rate, and temperature) before an illness occurs so you will know what is normal for your dog.

- **Pulse**

  - Normal pulse-rate is 80-140 per minute. In large or old dogs the pulse is generally slower.

  - Fast pulse is characteristic of shock.

  - Weak pulse is a serious sign.

  - Pulse may be checked in an area where an artery is near the surface. A good spot is the inside of the hind leg where the leg joins the body.

- **Respiration Rate**

  - The normal respiratory rate range is 10-30 per minute. Count either the expirations or inspirations, but not both.

- **Temperature**

  - The normal temperature range is approximately 100° to 103°F. or 38° to 39°C.

MEDICAL HANDBOOK

- To help you recognize symptoms, diseases, and to perform simple first aid, it is wise to purchase a good home veterinary handbook.

- Ask your veterinarian to recommend one for you.

ARTIFICIAL RESPIRATION

- If the dog has stopped breathing from any cause, start artificial respiration immediately. Sometimes it is necessary to continue artificial respiration for 30 to 60 minutes.

  - **Chest Pressure Method**

    1. On a firm surface, lay dog on his right side.

    2. Pull tongue forward.

    3. Remove any foreign objects in throat.

    4. Press down firmly on ribs behind the shoulder.

    5. Release quickly.

    6. Repeat steps four and five at the rate of 12 times per minute.

- **Mouth-to-Muzzle Method**

    1. Pull tongue forward.

    2. Check for foreign objects.

    3. Hold the dog's mouth closed.

    4. Blow firmly into nostrils (20 per minute).

    5. Continue until the breathing is natural.

    6. If a veterinarian's assistance is necessary, continue resuscitation en route.

BANDAGE OR WOUND PROTECTION

- To prevent a dog from removing a bandage or licking a wound, construct a lightweight protection called an "Elizabethan Collar."

- From heavy cardboard, cut a collar from one of the two patterns shown below. Punch holes as indicated, place over dog's head, and lace together with a cord.

PATTERNS

Cone Collar　　　Elizabethan

- If your dog has to wear a dressing, rub Bitter Apple, citronella or Tabasco Sauce on the bandage to discourage removal.

BLACK TONGUE

- This disease is of dietary origin and not as common as formerly due to the availability of balanced commercial dog food.

- Characterized by inflammation and ulceration of the lips, throat, and tongue. As disease worsens, black discoloration appears. Saliva is thick, fetid, and often tinged with blood.

- Omit starchy food. Feed meat, liver, vegetables, soft-boiled eggs, and cottage cheese. Give vitamins even after the disease disappears in order to prevent recurrence.

BLEEDING

- Spurting, bright red blood indicates a cut artery. This is very serious. Place a sterile pad on the wound and apply pressure. Time is of the essence, so press your fingers directly on the wound if a pad is not available. Take dog to your veterinarian immediately.

Remember what you read
In that First-Aid book?
Don't try to be the doctor
No matter how I look.

- Venous bleeding is slow and dark red in color. Apply a tight bandage to the wound.

- Cold packs may slow bleeding.

- **Internal Bleeding**

  - Symptoms of shock are present.

  - Bleeding from the lungs and stomach is indicated by bright red blood coughed or vomited.

  - High intestinal bleeding will cause stools to be black.

  - Low intestinal tract bleeding will be indicated by stools mixed with bright red blood.

- **Tourniquet**

  - INTELLIGENT USE AND UNDERSTANDING OF ITS FUNCTION ARE ABSOLUTELY VITAL.

  - Improvised tourniquets can be made from ties, stockings, belts, or strips of material.

  - The tourniquet should be placed close to the wound and between it and the heart. Never use for a head or neck injury.

  - Should be tight enough to control the bleeding.

  - Loosen the tourniquet every 10 minutes for 3 to 4 minutes. Take your dog to the veterinarian immediately.

BROKEN OR FRACTURED LIMB

- Wrap the leg firmly in a towel, newspaper, or magazine as a temporary splint before transporting to the veterinarian.

  I broke my leg
  And I need help.
  Excuse me please
  If I have to yelp.

- Apply ice packs to decrease swelling and inflammation.

BURNS

- **Acid**   Burns caused by car batteries and some metal cleaners. Rinse with a solution of one teaspoon of baking soda to one quart of water.

- **Alkali**   Burns caused by cleaning products, grease dissolvers, drain openers, etc. Rinse with plain water or wash with water and vinegar rinse. SEE Vinegar, page 103.

- **Severe Burns**

  1. Do not apply ANY ointments.

  2. Soak sterile bandage in cold water and apply to burn.

3. Do not give any stimulent, sedative, or drug.

4. Keep patient quiet and warm.

5. See veterinarian immediately.

- **Superficial Burn**

   1. Immerse the burned area in cold water. Dry gently. Bandage with sterile dressing.

   2. Keep patient quiet and warm.

CAR ACCIDENT

- Even if your dog can walk away from a car accident, he should be examined by a veterinarian. If he is weak and has pale gums, he may be bleeding internally.

   If I'm hit by a car
   The best thing yet
   Is to keep me warm
   And call my vet.

- Bleeding from the nostrils may indicate a head injury.

- If your dog is in pain, muzzle him with a belt, tie, etc. Slip a board under him before transporting.

- Do not feed for the first 24 hours as the dog may vomit and start internal bleeding.

- Reduce the danger of blood clots for the next four days by avoiding too much exercise and feeding lighter and softer meals.

CHOKING

- Attempt to remove the foreign object with your fingers. Act quickly so that the object doesn't slip further back into the throat.

- If a thread is hanging out of the mouth, DO NOT remove as it may be attached to a needle. Take your dog to a veterinarian.

- If obstruction cannot be removed by the fingers, try the Heimlich Method: With the dog on his side, press firmly with both hands in the area of the last ribs. Release and repeat several times. The object should pop out.

COLD PACK

- Helps reduce edema fluid and control bleeding and pain by constricting the capillaries. DO NOT use on an injury more than 12-24 hours old. Ice cubes in a plastic bag and wrapped in a towel serves as a cold pack.

COLDS AND CONGESTION

- A running nose and breathing difficulties are signs of distemper. If no other symptoms are present, however, it may be just a cold caused by exposure.

- If the dog has pneumonia, he should be kept in a room that is warm and moist.

- For pneumonia, chest infection, or colds, a vaporizer and a couple of drops of tincture of benzine or camphor in the water is beneficial.

  - If no vaporizer is available, substitute a pan of boiling water on the stove.

  - Place dog in a bathroom. Run the shower or tub until the room is damp.

- Put a little Vicks Vapor Rub on his nose. He will lick it off and the camphor will help him breathe more freely.

- An ultraviolet sunlamp is helpful but protect his eyes.

- If the dog must be taken outdoors in cold weather, pin a small blanket across his chest or put a sweater on him.

CONJUNCTIVITIS

- This is an inflammation of the membrane of the eyelids caused by dust, smoke, foreign material, or is a sign of general illness.

    - Bathe the eyes three times a day with a 2 percent boric acid solution.

    - Boil one pint of water with one teaspoon of salt. Cool and bathe the eyes three times daily.

    - Keep the dog in a subdued light.

    - If the condition does not clear up in a few days, see your veterinarian.

CONSTIPATION

- Milk of Magnesia is a safe laxative. SEE Drug Dosage, page 101.

- Add more roughage to the diet.

- Blockage may be caused by a tumor or a foreign object. If constipation continues, see the veterinarian.

- Constipation often occurs in rainy or cold weather when the dog's only thought is to get back into the warm house. Insert a glycerine suppository before taking your dog for a walk.

- An enema of tepid water and mild soap suds may be necessary if purgatives are too slow acting or not advisable.

- For mild constipation, suppositories are often just as effective as an enema. Glycerine suppositories may be purchased from a pharmacy. Suppositories can also be made from a cake of soap by cutting it into pencil-shaped slivers.

- Mild constipation may be relieved by adding mineral oil to the food once a day. Warning: Do not continue for more than four days as it prevents the absorption of many valuable vitamins and minerals.

- WARNING! Never give a dog the cascara compound used for humans. It contains strychnine. ALWAYS CHECK LABELS ON MEDICATION.

COUGHS

- Coughing may be an indication of a serious problem. Observe your dog closely and report to the veterinarian.

- Vicks Salve is soothing to the throat. If placed on the nose of the dog, he will lick it off.

CUTS

- Cuts, abrasions, and scratches should be treated with soap and water.

- Instant medicated aerosol may be used on a cut or sore. The wound clears up quickly as the dog does not irritate it with constant licking.

- If a long-haired dog has a deep cut and no equipment is available, tie the long hair on each side of the cut to pull the skin together as close as possible.

DEHYDRATION

- Abnormal loss of body fluid through vomiting and diarrhea can cause dehydration. To check progress of dehydration, pinch the skin at the spine into a fold. If the fold stays stiffly up instead of returning to normal position, the dog is seriously dehydrated. See your veterinarian at once.

- After diarrhea or vomiting is under control, fluid must be replaced.

  - Boil hamburger in salted water and remove fat. Feed small amounts several times a day.

- Give the dog a small amount of water mixed with a pinch of salt or soda. If the dog can keep this down, continue every half hour for four hours.

- Give honey and water.

- Doughnuts are excellent as they provide sugar and help coax the appetite.

- Until ready for regular food, feed chicken and rice soup with bread.

DIARRHEA

- **Causes**

  1. Allergies to certain foods
  2. Internal parasites
  3. Poisons
  4. Radical change of diet
  5. Spicy and cold food
  6. Stress
  7. Tainted food
  8. Too much fat

  If humans have the "trots"
  They head for a facility.
  We poor canines just hold it
  To the best of our ability.

- **Treatment**

  - Withhold food and water for 24-36 hours.

  - Give Kaopectate or Pepto-Bismol. SEE Drug Dosage, page 101.

  - After a 24-hour fast, feed the dog small amounts of bland food frequently. SEE Bland Diets, page 39.

  - Gradually switch to regular diet.

DISLOCATION

- In a dislocation of a hip or knee, there is loss of movement and often swelling. Put cold compresses on the area immediately and see your veterinarian.

EAR CANKER

- Internal ear canker is caused by water, dirt, parasites, or eczema.

- External ear canker is caused by cuts, dog bites, or bruises on the ear flap. If the dog rubs or paws his ear, the problem is intensified.

- Ulcers or raw spots may appear in the ear canal.

- Symptoms of an ear canker are a hot and swollen ear, dark discharge, foul or almond-like odor.

- Clean the ear daily and apply a mild antiseptic lotion. If this does not clear up the problem see your veterinarian.

EAR CARE

- Clean, dry ears seldom cause problems.

- If there is an ear problem in a long-eared dog, tape the ears to the top of the head to allow air to circulate freely.

- To clean, soak a cloth in mineral oil and wipe out the ear.

- For better air circulation in long-eared dogs, keep inside of ear shaved.

- If a dog has been playing in tall grass and weeds, check for foreign objects that may be in the ear canal.

- Prevent water from getting into the ear when bathing.

- If your dog continues to show signs of distress after several days (such as shaking the head, whimpering, or refusing to eat) take him to the veterinarian for examination.

EAR MITES

- **Symptoms**

  - Dog shakes his head or rubs the affected ear.

  - A dark, waxy material is found in the ear canal.

  - If in doubt, have it diagnosed by a veterinarian.

- **Treatment**

  - Clean ears with cotton dipped in alcohol, hydrogen peroxide, or mineral oil.

  - Apply ear-mite preparation such as "Canex," Ridamite," or "Pelene."

ELECTRIC SHOCK

- FIRST, disconnect cord.

- Administer artificial respiration if necessary. SEE Artificial Respiration, page 46.

  The luscious cord
  From lamp to wall —
  If we bite into that
  We're due for a fall.

- Give a whiff of ammonia.

- Call the veterinarian immediately.

- IF CONSCIOUS, give a little whiskey or coffee.

EYE INJURIES

- Place a bandage over the eye to prevent movement of the eye. Take your dog to the veterinarian immediately.

- Prevent your dog from scratching eyes by one of the following methods:

  - Tape the feet together so your pet can walk but cannot scratch at the injury and cause further harm.

- Tape socks on the feet.

- If a dog has dewclaws (extra toe on inside of leg), tape them to the leg so the eyes will not be harmed from scratching.

- Use the Elizabethan collar made from a sheet of cardboard with hole cut for the head. (SEE Bandage and Wound Protection, page 47.)

EYE IRRITATION

- The dog's eyes may become irritated by air pollution, chemicals, dust, soap, or sprays. Dip sterile cotton in warm water and squeeze into the eye until the irritants are flushed away. If this does not bring relief, see your veterinarian.

- Commercial eye drops also relieve minor eye irritation.

FEET

- **Cracked and Sore Pads**

  - Apply bag balm. May be purchased at drug or farm supply stores.

  - Epsom salts in hot water is excellent for swollen paws. Soak three times a day for ten minutes.

  - Soak the dog's feet twice a day in water made pink by a few grains of permanganate of potash. (Obtain at drug store.) After soaking feet, cover with bandage, and tape with adhesive.

- **Soaking**

  - A plastic rain-boot is helpful if the injured pad must be treated by soaking in a medicated solution. It eliminates the problem of keeping the dog's foot in a bowl of medication.

FEVER

- Fever may be an indication of a serious problem. Observe your dog carefully for other symptoms. Consult your veterinarian.

- A fever causes the dog to be thirsty but drinking water usually results in vomiting. A good idea is to place several ice cubes in the drinking bowl instead of water.

FITS AND CONVULSIONS

- If your pet ever suffers from a fit, convulsions, hysteria, or similar evidence of illness, throw a blanket over him to limit his movement so he will not injure himself.

- Attacks may last from only a few minutes to half an hour.

- If the dog is outside, take him into the house as soon as possible.

- Apply cold water or cracked ice to the back of the head. Then rub the back of his head where it joins the neck.

- Attacks may indicate a serious illness. See your veterinarian promptly.

FLATULENCE (GAS)

- **Cause**

  - Gas may result from a diet high in meat, eggs, starchy or spicy food, gulping food (thus swallowing air), cottage cheese, too much fat, or vegetables in the cabbage family.

- **Treatment**

  - Charcoal pills after eating may help.

  - Give Milk of Magnesia. SEE Dosage, page 101.

  - Try buttermilk on the food. Give one cup, daily, for a large dog.

FOREIGN OBJECTS

- **Fish Hooks**

    - Cut off the barbs with pliers, then PUSH the hook through gently.

    - Hooks that are deeply imbedded should be attended to by a veterinarian.

    You aren't a veterinarian
    So don't get carried away.
    Do what you must
    And call him without delay.

- **Grass Seed in Nose**

    - Grass seed lodged high in the dog's nostril can cause alarming symptoms similar to distemper. Contact your veterinarian immediately.

- **Imbedded Objects**

    - If an object such as a stick, nail, or metal shaft, is deeply imbedded, it may cause severe internal damage. Leave object in place for removal in the veterinary hospital.

    - Keep the dog as immobile as possible to prevent further injury.

- **Porcupine Quills**

    - Porcupine quills can be more easily removed if softened with vinegar before pulling out.

    - Be sure all quills are removed. An imbedded quill could work through the body. Remove those near vital areas first.

    - Removal of quills is quite painful. Before you begin, give your dog a mild sedative. If that is not available, aspirin will help.

- **Swallowed Foreign Objects**

  - If your dog swallows a sharp article and you are not where you can get to a veterinarian immediately, the following suggestions will help prevent internal injury.

    - Mix pieces of raw hamburger in cotton and feed to the dog. The hamburger in cotton helps cushion the object and passes out in three or four days with the stool.

    - Immediately feed bread, potatoes, or any soft food to help cushion the foreign object.

    - If a dog swallows any foreign object, watch him carefully for several days. If he vomits or becomes constipated, take him to veterinarian.

FROSTBITE

- For frostbite, a slow, steady, moist heat is the best treatment. Bathe the afflicted part with tepid water first. Gradually increase the water temperature. Do not exceed 102°.

HEAT STROKE OR PROSTRATION

- **Symptoms**

  - Panting

  - Frothing at the mouth

  - Pale or gray gums

  - Vomiting

  - Abnormal and rapid breathing

  - High temperature (about 107°F. or 41 + 5C)

  - Muscle spasms

  - Collapse

- **Treatment**

  - Place dog in a cool spot.

  - Keep the dog in a prone position with tongue pulled forward so that he does not swallow it and choke.

  - Cold towels may be placed on the body and head.

  - Submerge dog in a tub of cold water.

  - A cool enema will reduce temperature.

  - DO NOT LOWER BODY TEMPERATURE TOO SUDDENLY. Check with thermometer every 3 to 5 minutes until the temperature is normal.

  - If dog is CONSCIOUS, give a small amount of water.

  - Take dog to veterinarian immediately.

HICCUPS

- Are usually normal and common in young puppies but may be a sign of a dietary problem or worms.

HOT COMPRESSES

- Hot compresses are used for a deep or superficial infection, abscess, bruise, or muscular injury OVER 12 HOURS OLD.

- Hot packs aid in the removal of edema fluid and swelling.

INSECT BITES AND STINGS

- Remove stinger.

- A sting in the mouth can cause swelling and the throat can close. Use ice to keep swelling down and rush your pet to a veterinarian.

Minding my own business
Relaxing under the trees
Along came to buzz and sting
A whole swarm of bees.

- Some dogs are very allergic to bee stings so it is wise to have antihistamine, recommended by your veterinarian, available in your First Aid Kit.

- To alleviate the pain, mix ¼ teaspoon of meat tenderizer with one teaspoon of water and apply to sting. This preparation eases the pain and breaks down the poison.

KENNEL COUGH

- Is a harsh, dry cough that is a mild and self-limiting disease but contagious.

- Isolate your dog.

- The incubation period is between five to ten days.

- Your vet will prescribe a relief for the coughing.

- Vaccination for prevention is available from your veterinarian.

MOVING INJURED DOG

- An injured dog should be placed on a board. Do not lift but gently slip a board under him.

- A temporary stretcher could also be made by taking a blanket and rolling the edges.

- In an emergency, a rug, or a box can substitute for a stretcher.

NETTLES

- Nettles are highly irritating. antihistamine may be recommended by your veterinarian.

- To relieve the intense itching, bathe dog in cold water with vinegar. Mix two quarts of water to one pint of vinegar.

POISON

- If in doubt whether a substance is poisonous, call the Poison Control Center.

Skull and crossbone things
Are high upon a shelf.
A good thing I can't reach them
Or I'd surely harm myself.

- Poisoning occurs in four ways: absorption, ingestion, inhalation, and injection.

  - **Absorption**

    - Occurs when dog comes in contact with a poisonous substance such as acid, alkali, or insecticides which gets on the skin and is then absorbed into the body.

    - Remove the substance by bathing and rinsing.

  - **Ingestion**

    - Early symptoms are salivation, retching, vomiting, tensing of the abdomen, and roaching of the back.

    - Symptoms in the ADVANCE STAGE are collapse, muscle spasms, paralysis, slow breathing, bleeding from body openings, and bloody urine.

    - Remove any foreign matter from the mouth. A rough cloth will pick up the small pieces easier.

    - Keep the dog quiet and warm.

    - DO NOT INDUCE VOMITING IF DOG HAS INGESTED A CAUSTIC SUBSTANCE. Any substance capable of burning, corroding, or destroying living tissue is caustic, this includes alkali, petroleum products or acid. Dilute the poison by giving water or milk if dog is conscious.

    - For NON-CAUSTIC poisoning, induce vomiting with large quantities of Hydrogen Peroxide mixed with equal parts of water. SEE page 48 for other emetics.

- The next step is to give raw eggs and milk to dilute the poison and act as a coating agent. NOT TO BE USED FOR POISONS CONTAINING PHOSPHORUS.

- Take the dog and poisonous substance immediately to the veterinarian. Include any vomitus and feces.

- IMMEDIATE VETERINARIAN ATTENTION IS ESSENTIAL FOR INGESTED CAUSTIC AND NON-CAUSTIC POISONING.

- Inhalation

  - If dog has been exposed to toxic fumes such as airplane glue, cleaning fluid, gas, lacquer thinner, or smoke, take him to the fresh air immediately and apply artificial respiration. SEE page 46.

- Injection

  - Injected poisoning occurs when a dog has an allergic reaction to drugs, vaccines, insect bites, snake bites, and toad poisoning.

  - Remove the offending object, clean the area, and apply cold packs to reduce swelling.

  - If the reaction is severe, it may be necessary to perform artificial respiration and seek professional care.

  - Snake bite and treatment, SEE page 65.

  - Toad poisoning and treatment, SEE page 67.

SHOCK

- Symptoms

  - Shallow breathing   *Keep me warm and dry*
  - Nervousness   *And quickly call the vet.*
  - Pale gums   *With a problem like this*
  - Collapse   *He's our very best bet.*

- **Treatment**

  - Put the dog's head lower than his body. Cover him with a warm blanket and a heating pad against the blanket.

  - Keep him quiet.

  - If the dog is conscious, give him warm water or milk with a little sugar.

  - As soon as the dog can swallow, mix a small amount of brandy with an equal amount of honey or sugar. Give one-half teaspoonful (or one-half eyedropper full) directly into the dog's mouth and rub his throat to encourage swallowing. If color is slow in returning to the mouth and gums, give another dose in a few minutes.

SNAKEBITE

- Usually two fang marks indicate a poisonous snake. U-shaped teeth marks are left by non-poisonous snakes.

  - Immobilize and calm animal.

  - Muzzle the dog; snake bites are extremely painful and your dog may turn on you.

  - Remove the venom by cutting into the wound and suck wound with mouth. Do not swallow.

- Apply a tourniquet between the bite and the heart. Release every 15 minutes for one-minute intervals.

- Clean the wound with soap and water (or wash with full-strength hydrogen peroxide), dry, and apply an ice pack.

- Do not give a stimulant of any kind.

- Take the dog to a veterinarian immediately for an anti-venin shot.

SPRAINS

- In the first few hours after the injury, apply an ice pack. Leave it on the swollen joint for 10 to 15 minutes every two hours.

- Rest the injured joint or leg. Splinting may be necessary.

STINGS

- SEE Insect and Bee Stings, page 61.

TAILS

- To protect a tail so it can heal, place gauze over wound and bandage with a thick roll of cotton wrapped with adhesive tape.

- If the skin is broken, clean with a disinfectant and apply medicated ointment.

- If tail is broken or partially severed, take the dog to a veterinary hospital.

THERMOMETERS

- Use an ordinary rectal thermometer. Sterilize with alcohol, then dip in petroleum jelly or moisten the end with soapy water. Insert three-quarters of the thermometer into the anus and leave for two minutes.

- A new product called Canine Clinitemp, a fever detector, makes it easy to find a dog's temperature. It is a small plastic strip which should be pressed firmly onto your dog's lower abdomen. In 60 seconds, you will get a reading.

TOAD POISONING

- Certain species of toads found in the south produce a potent toxin from the salivary glands. If your dog has mouthed one of these toads, the poison can produce symptoms of fast breathing, rapid heartbeat, drooling, and seizures. Contact with these particular toads can be fatal unless emergency treatment is given.

- Wash dog's face with a large amount of cool water.

- Give artificial respiration if necessary.

- Wrap dog in blanket to maintain heat.

- Take your dog to the veterinarian immediately.

URINE RETENTION

- This problem has many causes. Sometimes it is as simple as inclement weather when the dog prefers a warm house to the harsh elements. However, obesity, chills, bladder, kidney stones, or a toxic condition may be the cause.

- Give ten drops of potassium nitrate mixed with two teaspoons of water every thirty minutes for one and and one-half hours. If, after this time, there are no results, consult your veterinarian immediately.

VOMITING

- **Causes**

    - Dogs can vomit at will and it is not always a cause for alarm. However, if the vomiting continues see your veterinarian immediately. Waste no more time with home remedies.

- Vomiting may be caused by distemper, hepatitis, kidney disease, leptospirosis, metritis, and pancreatitis.

- Some other causes for vomiting are allergy, attention-getting, car sickness, change of diet, constipation, excessive food, excitement, grass-eating, heatstroke, hunger, jealousy, obstruction, poison, or worms.

- A serious consequence of vomiting is dehydration.

- **Treatment**

  - Withhold all food and water for 24 hours.

  - Give one to two teaspoons of water if dog is very thirsty.

  - After vomiting has stopped, feed small amount of broth, boiled egg, rice, cereal, or boiled hamburger every two to four hours.

  - Give Kaopectate, Maalox, Mylanta, or Pepto-Bismol.

- **Vomiting — Emetic**

  - CAUTION: Do NOT induce vomiting if dog has swallowed acid, alkali, petroleum products, or a sharp object.

  - Quick action is necessary to prevent poisons from entering the blood stream if the dog has ingested anti-freeze, lead, rat poison, herbicide, etc.

  - Induce vomiting if the dog has *recently* swallowed objects such as socks, cloth, cleaning pads, rocks, etc.

  - If animal is conscious, use one of the following emetics:

    1. Hydrogen peroxide (3%) full strength or diluted.

    2. One teaspoon of table salt in one cup of warm water.

    3. One tablespoon of powdered mustard in one cup of warm water.

GROOMING

Mirror, mirror, on the wall
I'm the handsomest of them all.
Brushes and combs, don't you agree
Have created a new image of me.

BATHING TIPS

- **Clogged Pipes**

  - If you bathe your dog in a bathtub or shower, put steel wool over the drain to prevent hairs from clogging the pipes.

  - Another way to save a plumber's bill is to take a piece of nylon net and place in the drain. The water runs out easily but hair won't slip through.

- **Control**

  - A chain collar on the dog while bathing will give you more control.

  - Tie the dog with a nylon cord to the *cold* water faucet.

- **Dry Clean**

  - If for some reason, such as illness, cold weather, etc., you do not wish to bathe your dog, dry clean him. Buy a commercial product or use oatmeal, bran, or cornmeal. Apply and brush it out. A sheet on the floor under the grooming table will eliminate a messy clean up.

- **Drying Dog**

  - A wet chamois, well wrung out, will absorb far more water than a cloth or a towel.

  - To prevent matting of hair, blot and squeeze water from coat. Do not rub dry.

- **Ear Protection**

  - Placing your finger against the dog's ear canal will protect the ear from water while bathing or rinsing.

  - Put cotton in the dog's ears before bathing.

- **Eye Protection**

  - A drop of mineral oil in the dog's eyes will keep the soap from stinging.

  - Apply vaseline around the eyes before bathing.

    Every time you draw my bath
    You rouse my deepest fears.
    I cannot stand for soap
    To run into my eyes or ears.

- **Frequency**

  - Experts differ as to the number of baths to give a dog.

  - Frequency of baths should be determined by circumstances and breed differences.

  - Bathing dries the skin and coat and results in shedding.

  - Baths ARE needed to remove filth and control parasites.

- **Matting**

  - The dog's coat will mat if you wash the dog like you shampoo your hair. Wet the dog thoroughly, then squeeze the shampoo through the coat. Rinse well.

- **Overlooked Areas**

  - The two most commonly overlooked spots when bathing a dog are the rectal area and the pads of the feet. Scrub both places well, using a small hand brush.

    When you're giving me a bath
    There's a place you musn't fail.
    In order to be delicate
    We'll call it under the tail.

- **Pesticidal Shampoo**

  - A harmless shampoo that actually KILLS fleas! It is inexpensive and is one you can make yourself. Completely removes dirt yet doesn't dry the skin or coat. Clears up minor skin irritations.

    Mix thoroughly: 1 cup of kerosene, 2 cups of Ivory Snow and 2½ quarts of water.

  Pour mixture over the dog and squeeze into the coat. Leave on for ten to fifteen minutes. Rinse thoroughly.

- **Procedures**

  - Brush and comb away all mats in the coat before bathing. Mats that remain damp could cause skin irritation.

  - Water should be lukewarm and no higher than the dog's stomach. Do not put dog in tub until the water is at the correct level as sound of water coming out of the faucet is disturbing to your dog.

  - Soap around the neck first. This prevents body fleas from moving and hiding in the ears.

- **Rinsing**

  - In most instances, the harmful effect of bathing a dog is due to the use of irritating soaps and inadequate rinsing. The residue of soaps can cause intense itching and scratching.

  - Rinsing a dog in a tub of clear water does not remove all the soap residue. If at all possible, use a spray for rinsing soap out of the coat. If one is not available, pour rinse water over the dog using a bottle or a pan.

- **Shampoo**

  - Disinfectants and lye in some soaps may cause skin irritation.

  - Liquid soap with coconut oil or a similar base is preferable to bar soap.

  - Frequent use of detergents has a drying effect on the skin and hair.

  - Woolite is an excellent shampoo to brighten your dog's coat.

- **Slippery Tub**

  - To prevent slipping, put a heavy towel or rubber bath mat in the bottom of the tub. The dog will feel more secure.

- **Soda Rinse**

  - Add baking soda to rinse water to help remove soap and soothe the skin.

- **Soda Sponge Bath**

  - If your dog rolls in smelly, filthy dirt, rub him with a damp sponge sprinkled heavily with baking soda. Follow the rub down with a rinse in clear water.

COATS

- **Brushing**

  - To keep the dog clean between baths, brush frequently. This keeps the hair in good condition by stimulating the skin and removing dead hair.

    I become ecstatic when
    I see you're going to brush.
    Don't miss any places
    And don't get in a rush.

  - When you brush, do not skip around from one area to another. Do each section thoroughly.

- Troubled by the fine hairs around the back of the ears? A wig brush, available at drug stores, is effective in brushing and separating these hairs. The brush is, however, too harsh for regular use on the rest of the body.

- **Clipping**

    - In summer the coats of long-haired dogs should be thinned or trimmed. Never shave a dog unless it is necessary for treatment of a skin disease.

- **Dampen Coats**

    - Use a spray bottle filled with water to moisten the coat before and during brushing. Damp hair is more manageable, and the brush or comb passes through the coat more easily. There is less chance of breaking the hair.

- **Dry Coat and Shedding**

    - Keep a dog's coat and skin soft and oily by mixing equal parts of olive oil and bay rum. Apply a small amount daily with a spray bottle and lightly towel. Expecially good when coat is dry and shedding is excessive.

    - Same procedure as above but use one capful of Keri Body Lotion to a pint spray bottle full of water.

        Brush me tender,
        Brush me do,
        And less of my fur
        You'll find on you.

    - When removing shedding coats, rub Vaseline Hair Tonic well into the coat before and while combing the dog.

    - Cleaning attachments of your vacuum cleaner used on your dog's coat will pick up loose hair and even a flea or two.

    - Is the dog dropping coat? If you have given up shows for a while, then give him a warm bath to hasten the process. This will free the dead hair and hasten the new growth. BRUSH BEFORE BATHING.

- **Mats and Tangles**

  - Work mats and tangles loose with fingers and a wet tooth comb; a drop of vegetable oil may help.

  - Commercial products are available in pet supply stores which help to work out mats and tangles.

  - Use thinning shears to cut out mats and tangles. Cut INTO the mat several times. Take a comb and gently comb downward. The mat combs right out with none of the disfigurement caused by regular scissors.

- **Soft Coats**

  - Coats which are soft, fine, and profuse should not be subjected to vigorous rubbing. After the bath, blot gently to prevent matting and pulling of the hair. There will be less tangling.

  - If dog's hair is too fine and soft, saturate the coat with beer to make it coarser and stiffer.

- **Thinning Hair**

  - Patches of shedding or thinning hair could be the result of a malfunctioning thyroid gland or a tumor on one of the endocrine glands. Have your veterinarian give your dog a thorough examination.

EARS

- **Cleaning**

  - Cotton tips for cleaning are dangerous in the hands of inexperienced people as dirt and wax may be pushed further into the ear.

- Use a cotton ball moistened with alcohol. This
does the job well and the
alcohol will evaporate
quickly. This is especially
helpful for long-eared
dogs.

Go easy poking
  Around in my ears...
I need the things
  In order to hear.

- Your dog's ears should be cleaned regularly but not with
water. Try baby oil or mineral oil for soothing and gentle
cleansing.

- **Plucked Hair**

  - Some breeds, such as poodles and Lhasa apsos, need hair
  plucked out of ears; otherwise, ear care should not extend
  beyond wiping the outermost portion of the ear with a
  moistened ball of cotton.

- **Water Dogs**

  - If your dog does water work, put a couple drops of mineral
  or baby oil in the ears two or three times a week. This will
  help to keep ears free of infection.

  - To permit better air circulation in long-eared dogs, clip or
  shave hair from the inside of the ear folds.

EYES

- **Eye Stain**

  - To remove normal eye stain caused by tearing, obtain a
  commercial product at a pet supply store or make your own
  preparation. Add one teaspoon of Boric Acid in one cup of
  warm water and apply.

- **Soothing**

  - When a dog's eyes become irritated by wind, dust, or chalk
  he pulls up the haw (third eyelid) thus changing his expres-
  sion. Soothe the eyes by applying Murine or Visine.

EQUIPMENT

- **Brushes**

  - **Bristle**   Recommended for short, medium, and long-coated breeds.

  - **Pin**   Has straight teeth. Recommended for long silky-coated breeds.

  - **Rubber**   Ideal for polishing the coats of smooth-coated breeds.

  - **Slicker**   Has bent teeth. Recommended for use on medium-coated breeds — particularly poodles.

- **Cleanup**

  - **Holder**   Install a paper holder in your kennel, whelping room, etc. It's cheaper than facial tissue and can do a good job cleaning ears, eyes, and small wipe-ups.

  - **Sponge**   A damp sponge readily picks up the loose hair on the grooming table, equipment, and clothes.

- **Combs**

  - **Coarse**   Used for dense and heavy coats.

  - **Fine**   Suggested for soft, sparse, or silky hair.

  - **Medium**   Used for average-length coats.

- **Hair Dryers**

  - Dryers will not cause coats to snarl which often happens by improper towel drying.

  - To prevent colds in the winter, use a hair dryer to hasten the drying process.

- Different model hair dryers may be purchased to suit your particular need: hand, cage, table, or stand.

- **Metal Equipment Care**

  - All tools should be dry before storing.

  - To prevent rusting, put lubricating oil or vaseline on a rag and rub over the tools when the grooming session is finished.

  - Rust spots can be removed with Naval Jelly.

- **Mitt for Grooming**

  - A piece of short piled carpet with a loop to hold on the hand, or made into a mitt, is an excellent aid for grooming smooth coats. It scratches enough to rub off the loose hair but is not harsh enough to harm the skin.

  I'm handsome,
  Jaunty and debonair.
  Girls, here I am
  You'd better beware

- **Pockets**

  - A carpenter's apron with numerous pockets to hold combs, brushes, scissors, and treats, makes grooming easier.

  - Smocks are often used by professional groomers because of the large pockets which are handy for equipment.

- **Scissors**

  - Barber shears have long straight blades which taper to a point. They are used for overall scissoring.

  - Blunt-tipped scissors have curved blades and rounded tips. They are used for scissoring around feet. It is advisable to use them on wiggly puppies.

  - Nasal scissors have a short straight blade with a ball tip. This type is used for whiskers and between toes.

- Shears, Thinning

  - Thinning shears are used for thinning long or thick hair. They may also be used to cut out mats and tangles.

  - There are two styles:

    1. The single-edged thinners have one serrated blade and one scissor blade.

    2. Double-edged thinners have two serrated blades.

  - Both types of thinners are made with different number of teeth. The single-edged shears, extra fine, are preferred as they produce a smoother finish.

  - Your choice of thinners is a matter of personal preference. Buy the best. They last longer and give better results.

- Storage

  - Tack boxes for grooming equipment and supplies can either be purchased or made. These boxes are divided into compartments and trays, making equipment easily accessible.

  - A canvas-type suitcase, lined with plastic, makes a convenient grooming kit.

  - A fishing tackle box, with its many divisions, can be organized into a very handy grooming kit.

- Table for Grooming

  - To make a grooming table, you will need:

Legs, folding	Purchase at hardware store
Plywood	2' x 3' x ¾'', round off corners
Rubber matting	Slip-resistant
Glue	Glue rubber to plywood before using trim
Edging	10' of ¾'' trim
Crutch tips	For the legs

- **Arm for Grooming Table**

  - A grooming arm can be purchased to clamp on the table. An inexpensive method, however, is to fasten a strong hook into the ceiling above the grooming table. Fasten one end of the leash to it.

FEET

- **Disinfect the Feet**

  - At dog shows or when exercising in public areas, your dog is exposed to many minor and perhaps serious diseases. After arriving home, disinfect each paw with a fairly strong solution of disinfectant. There are many good products on the market but Clorox, diluted according to directions, is excellent. Do NOT use a disinfectant which contains PHENOL or CARBOLIC ACID.

  - Roundworms can be easily contracted in public areas. Bathe your dog's feet in a solution of water and table salt to kill the worm eggs that may have adhered to the feet.

- **Ice and Snow**

  - If you walk dogs on ice and snow, make certain that the feet are washed and cleaned when you return home. Rock salt and chemicals used to melt snow can cause sore and aching pads. Soothe the pads by bathing in a solution of bicarbonate of soda.

- **Mats**

  - The pads of long-coated dogs should be checked frequently. Mats of hair and dirt get between the toes and pads. Unless it is removed it can be quite painful to the dog.

FOREIGN OBJECTS

- **Burrs**

  - Burrs in the coat can be more readily removed if they are first crushed with pliers.

  - A burr in the coat can be removed quickly by the use of a kitchen fork slipped under the burr.

  - If you find burrs in a dog's coat, soak the burrs in petroleum jelly or mineral oil before working them out.

  - Before running a long-haired dog in an area infested with burrs, rub warmed petroleum jelly or a few tablespoons of mineral oil into the dog's feathers, ears, and chest. Fewer burrs and unwanted material will accumulate and what does will be more easily brushed out.

- **Tar and Paint**

  - Tar and paint can be removed by saturating the substance with vegetable oil. Allow the vegetable oil to soak for several hours before shampooing your dog.

  - Do not use turpentine or kerosene to remove tar or paint as they may cause painful burns.

  - If tar is on the coat where the dog can chew it off, remove immediately as it is a toxic substance.

  - Road tar is painful if it gets on the pads or between the toes. Cut it out with scissors.

  - If you do not wish to cut out any hair, work vaseline into the tar or paint. Remove with a cloth. Repeat if necessary.

NAILS

- **Bleeding**

  - A good coagulator may be obtained at your drug store.

  - A styptic pencil will help to clot the blood.

  - Hydrogen peroxide is an excellent coagulator.

  - Ice applied to the nail will reduce bleeding.

  - Cornstarch is an inexpensive coagulator.

- **Cutting Nails**

  - If the dog's nails click when he is walking across a hard surface, the nails are too long. The nails should be about even with the bottom pad of the foot. When they tend to hook, they are much too long.

    On nail clipping day
    I'm really sad
    Because you think
    I'm acting so bad.

  - In a light-colored nail, it is easy to see the blood vessel and you can avoid cutting into it. In the dark nails, on the underside of the curve, you will find a small groove. To prevent bleeding, cut below the groove.

  - Nail clippers may be purchased at a pet supply store. If totally unfamiliar with the procedure, ask the salesperson, breeder, or veterinarian for a demonstration.

  - If you cut toenails right after a bath, it is easier to see the quick and easier to cut. Baby oil serves the same purpose.

- **Dry Nails**

  - Aged house dogs, particularly, can have dry, brittle, cracking toe nails. Unflavored gelatin powder added daily to their food (approximately one package per 100 pounds) works wonders.

SCHEDULE

- For a dog to always look his best and be comfortable and healthy, owners should maintain a weekly grooming schedule. Set up the schedule on your calendar.

SHORT-HAIRED DOGS

- Regular grooming removes loose hairs and keeps oil in the coat.

- Brush in the direction in which the hair grows.

- Use a chamois to give sheen to the coat.

TEETH

- Tartar is a hard, yellow or brown substance found on the teeth. Remove by taking a dime to crack and scrape off the tartar. A tartar scraper designed for this purpose may be purchased at pet supply stores.

- Tartar must be removed to prevent gum disease. If the dog objects, better let the veterinarian do it.

- Gly-Oxide available at drug stores helps clean teeth and soothe inflamed gums.

- Plaque on the teeth may be removed by brushing with a toothbrush or rubbing with a washcloth dipped in soda.

URINE ODOR

- Long-haired dogs often have this problem. Mix one teaspoon of five percent sodium hypochlorite to a gallon of water and spray sparingly as it has a bleaching effect.

KENNELING

All of us need
  To have a good home
That's quiet, and peaceful
  And completely our own.

BEDS

- **Bathtubs**

  - Bathtubs made for babies may be utilized as a bed. They are of heavy plastic, easy to keep clean, and reasonable in price. The walls stop drafts.

- **Benches**

  - In a kennel, the dog should have a sleeping bench raised off the floor.

- **Cardboard Cartons**

  - An inexpensive bed cut to size from a carton, makes a cuddly bed which doesn't have to be cleaned. If soiled — just burn and replace it.

- **Dog Crates**

  - Dog crates fitted with a pad make an excellent bed. They are easily cleaned, and the dog feels safe and secure.

  - The fiberglass crates come in two sections. These parts may be utilized as separate beds.

- **Foam Beds**

  - A cozy bed with soft foam sides, a vinyl bottom, and a separate foam cushion — all washable — may be purchased at pet supply stores.

- **Hammock or Lounge**

  - Made from heavy material and metal framing. It keeps dog off the cold cement or dirt floors and is clean and sanitary.

- **Horse Feed Tubs**

  - Plastic feed tubs made for horses are approximately two feet in diameter with sides ten inches high. They are very durable and can be easily cleaned with soap and water.

  I like to have a bed
  All my very own
  And when I'm in it,
  Please leave me alone.

- **Size**

  - Your dog will feel more secure if he can snuggle against the sides of his bed. It is, therefore, suggested that his bed be only slightly larger than he is.

- **Water Beds**

  - They are non-allergenic, easily cleaned, and great for arthritic or rheumatic dogs. May be obtained at many leading pet supply stores.

- **Wicker or Metal Baskets**

  - Check at pet supply stores for various styles. Many of them are fitted with foam mattresses.

BEDDING

  - Bedding for dog houses should never be old rugs and blankets as they absorb moisture. Wood shavings, straw, or marsh hay are preferred.

- **Cedar Mattress**

  - The use of cedar shavings for bedding makes the dogs smell nice, keeps their coat glossy, and discourages parasites.

- To make a cedar mattress, sew together heavy material with a zipper at one end. The zipper makes it easy to remove the shavings and wash the bed. The old cedar shavings can be used around flowers as mulch.

- **Foam Mattress**

  - Cut foam to the size of dog and cover with a washable material. Sew zipper at one end for ease in removing the cover.

- **Sleeping Bag, Discarded**

  - A soft mattress for your dog can be made from an old folded sleeping bag. Easy to launder.

BOARDING KENNELS

- Check boarding kennel thoroughly before leaving your dog. Inspect for cleanliness, security, and appearance of boarders. Contact referrals.

- If you have a barker, leave your dog in his own environment with a neighbor or friend to care for him.

- Inform the kennel management if dog has a medical problem. Leave medication with instructions.

- A very nervous dog could be given a mild tranquilizer to help him adjust more readily. Check with your veterinarian.

- Ask for permission to leave a favorite toy.

- Minimize the chance of disease by having all necessary vaccinations before taking your dog to the kennel.

- Leave number where you may be reached in case of an emergency; also name of your veterinarian.

CHAINING DOGS

- No one likes to chain a dog but if it must be, use a heavy chain that will not break when the dog gets excited.

- The chain should be 10 to 15 feet long.

- Injury can occur if the dog lunges while fastened to a heavy chain. Purchase a coil spring that can be fastened to the chain, thus absorbing part of the shock. Another method is to use an inner tube fastened to the unyielding chain.

- Do NOT put a choke collar on a chained dog.

- Do NOT chain a dog close to any barrier he could jump over. If the chain is not long enough, he could hang himself.

- SEE Dog Tender Reel and Dog on Trollies, pages 26 and 27.

CRATES

- Flooring

    - A non-skid bath mat makes excellent flooring for a crate. It can be removed and hosed off if necessary. If used on top of a crate, it will provide firm footing while grooming.

    - Indoor-outdoor carpeting applied with double-faced tape is a better method of carpeting crates than a throw rug that bunches up.

- Size

    - Crates should be large enough so that when standing the dog's head is able to touch the top.

      Be it ever so humble,
      This is my own pad,
      There's no inside plumbing,
      But it suits this canine lad.

    - If crate is too large, even a housebroken dog may dirty one corner away from the sleeping area rather than ask to be let out.

DISHES

- **Elevated Table**

  - A tall dog should eat from a raised surface to prevent neck and back problems. The table should be at a comfortable height for the individual dog. Cut holes in the top to hold the food and water dishes.

  - SEE Dishes, page 35.

- **Individual Dishes**

  - Dishes should be sterilized frequently.

  - Dishes can be identified by a numbering system or the dog's name.

  - Fingernail polish or colored tape can be used to identify dishes.

  - When buckets and dishes are taken out of the kennel runs to be cleaned, be sure the same utensil goes back to the same dog. This prevents spreading disease.

  - Different size or shaped bowls make identification easy.

- **Non-Mobile Dishes**

  - An outside water pan won't tip or be carried around the area if you use a tube pan made for an angel food cake. Drive a stake into the ground and place the tube pan over it.

- **No-Slip Dishes**

  - Glue a rubber jar ring to the bottom of the dish to prevent slipping. A rubber mat under the dish will serve the same purpose.

DOGHOUSE

- **Cleaning**

  - Clean doghouses regularly to prevent infestation of parasites. Use a strong salt solution or commercial cleaner.

- **Color**

  - When the outside temperature is approximately 90 degrees, a doghouse painted white is six to eight degrees cooler than a black doghouse.

- **Custom-Made Houses**

  - Plans for doghouses may be obtained from lumber yards or magazines. (Check READER'S GUIDE at the Library.) By making the house yourself, you can incorporate the best features. It can even be styled to match your own abode.

- **Door Sill**

  - Place a three or four inch high door sill over which the dog can step. This keeps drafts and snow from entering the house.

    I like my quarters
    Neat and clean
    Protected from the elements
    As I lie down and dream.

- **Doors**

  - Use two pieces of canvas. Overlap the edges by at least two inches.

  - The Indians and Frontiermen had fringe on the end of their buckskin hunting shirts so the water would run off easier and dry quicker. With this knowledge, comes an idea for a door. Cut strips of canvas in 2-inch strips to within four inches to the top of the material. (Pinking shears help to prevent the canvas from raveling.) It is wise to have three or four pieces a bit larger than the size of the opening. Place them on top of each other and fasten in or outside of the door either by tacks or a wire across. It is easy for the dog to enter or leave, but he will be well protected from the elements.

- **Material**

  - Purchase weatherproof plywood, at least one-half inch thick, to construct your doghouse. It weathers and lasts longer than ordinary plywood.

  - Wood shingles or siding nailed over plywood makes an attractive doghouse and provides excellent insulation.

- **Placement**

  - Do not place a doghouse IN a narrow run or near a fence. The dog might stand on the roof and jump over the fence.

  - Cut a hole IN the fence and place the doghouse OUTSIDE of the enclosure. Make the opening escape proof.

  - If practical, move doghouse periodically. This will help to control parasites.

- **Raised Houses**

  - Doghouses should be off the ground as a protection against dampness. A raised floor will not rot out as soon.

- **Roofs**

  - If kennel roof is tarred and sprinkled with dry cement, it will provide better protection against the weather.

  - Removable roofs make it easier to clean the doghouse and, if a dog becomes ill, you are better able to get to him for the attention he needs.

  - Dogs love a flat-roofed house to sit or lie on. It also keeps them off the damp ground.

- **Solar Heating**

  - Solar heating of doghouses and kennels is in its infancy but it is a factor to be taken into consideration.

- **Trunk**

  - An old trunk can be converted into a novel-looking, weather-proof, doghouse. Cut a door in the end.

FENCES

- Fences should be four feet high for small dogs and six feet for large ones. One-inch gauge fencing is recommended for small dogs as they cannot get their muzzles through it. One and one-half to two-inch gauge may be used for larger dogs.

  My master says that
  He'll find me a mate,
  I could get my own
  Except for this gate.

- It is possible to have a shorter fence if you use an 18-inch over-hang around the top.

- Fence gates should have a self-locking device.

- Never use redwood for fencing as it is poisonous. Should the dog chew on it, he could become very ill.

- Dogs are curious and hearing noises on the other side of a solid fence can cause barking and stress. Leave a narrow opening between the boards so they can see out.

- Manufacturers of kennel enclosures have wide selections of meshes, sizes, and accessories.

- A wide board or bricks sunk into the ground at the base of the fence will prevent diggers from escaping.

- Dig a trench 12'' x 18'' along the length of enclosure. Nail or fasten a two-foot strip of welded wire fencing to the base. Hold it in place with heavy rocks then cover with soil.

RUNS

- **Asphalt**

  - An asphalt surface is not as durable as concrete but has several advantages. It is easy to clean and the tar content repels wood ticks and various worm eggs. It is less abrasive to the dog's feet. Not recommended for hot climates.

- **Cement Runs**

  - Before pouring a cement run, spread several inches of commercial salt on the ground. Gently pour cement over the salt. The salt will control flea eggs on the ground, prevent weeds from growing in cracks, and cut down on odor of urine.

- **Cleaner Runs**

  - Spray dog runs several times a year with a good insecticide and a fungicide. Follow manufacturer's directions.

- **Disinfectant or Bleach Cleaning**

  - Give concrete or rock kennel runs an extra good cleaning by using a bleach or disinfectant. Mix with water and use in garden sprayer. It is less expensive than commercial kennel sprays. BE SURE RUNS ARE THOROUGHLY DRY BEFORE RETURNING DOGS TO AREA.

  - A simplified method of applying a disinfectant or a bleach to a concrete floor is to use a paint roller with a long handle.

  - BE SURE THE DISINFECTANT DOES NOT CONTAIN PHENOL OR CARBOLIC ACID.

- **Flame-Gun**

  - The use of a horticultural flame-gun has been found to reduce the number of parasitic ova on the concrete floor of a kennel run. It is fast, simple, and economical. There is no apparent damage to the floor.

- **Muddy Walkways**

  - Short, narrow strips of asphalt roofing pack down like blacktop if laid on top of muddy walkways.

- **Odor-Free Runs**

  - Runs of loose materials such as dirt, rock, gravel, etc. become sour or odorous from urine and fecal residue. Apply agricultural limestone monthly or as often as needed. A lawn spreader dispenses it properly although a shovel and coarse broom can do the work satisfactorily.

  - Two inches of sweet lime under three to four inches of pea gravel will eliminate odors when it is hosed down.

- **Pea Gravel**

  - Pea gravel is a low-cost ground cover which helps to develop good, tight feet on your dog.

- **Rough Surface**

  - When concrete is poured, tell the mason to brush or broom the surface, running the brush strokes with the pitch so water will be carried off. The rough surface allows the dogs to grip better with their toes — thus strengthening their feet.

- **Site**

  - Dogs need shade in hot weather. Place run where there are trees or construct a canvas overhang along the fence.

  - Do not build a run or dog house where it will annoy the neighbors.

- Do not place a run where the dog will be subjected to the teasing of passing children.

SEWAGE

- This problem depends on climate, kind of soil, and local restrictions.

- Dog Mini Septic Tanks may be purchased from pet supply stores.

- Digesters provide a sanitary and quick method of disposal for dog droppings.

- **Homemade Digester Information**

  - Lim'nate is a chemical to change solids to liquids.

  - Digesters must be installed where there is drainage.

  - Check local laws on distance of digesters from wells, lakes, streams, etc.

  - Lim'nate action stops in very cold weather so digester should be large enough to hold a build-up of stools.

  - Put ONLY stools in digesters, no inorganic matter.

- **Steel Drum Digester**

  - This digester handles the stools of three to four average-size dogs.

  - Materials needed:

    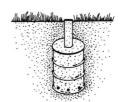

    - Steel drum — 55 gallons.

    - 6- or 8-inch drain tile.

    - Cover for tile should be tight to prevent flies.

- Installation:

    1. Cut hole in top of drum the same size as the bore of the drain tile.

    2. Drill 6 half-inch holes two inches from bottom of drum.

    3. Bury drum and fit tile over hole. Pack dirt around the tile to hold firmly in place.

- Use:

    1. Put droppings in drum.

    2. Once a week, add two tablespoons Lim'nate and four or five gallons of water.

    3. Fit cover over tile to keep out flies.

- **Tile Homemade Digester**

    - This type of digester will handle the stools of one large or two small dogs.

    - Procure a 10-inch bell sewer tile.

    - Bury the tile with bell end down. Make a tight fit-ting cover for the open end to prevent disease-spreading flies.

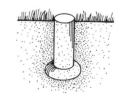

    - Put droppings in tile. Add one teaspoon of Lim'nate and two to three gallons of water once a week.

    - Enzyme action controls odors so there will be no complaints from neighbors.

    - Do not put inorganic objects in a digester as they will not liquefy.

WINTER CARE

- **Diet**

    - To help maintain body heat during cold weather, increase the daily allotment of food up to 25 percent.

    - At this season of the year, foods that are high in calories and fats are best.

- **Doghouse**

    - In cold climates, straw under and packed around the doghouse provides good insulation.

- **Hypothermia**

    - Ordinarily nature has provided the dog with sufficient coat to protect him against the cold. However, should the dog become injured and forced to remain in the cold without shelter for a long period of time he could suffer from hypothermia (lowering of body temperature).

    - Put the dog in a warm room, apply blankets and hot water bottles until the dog's temperature returns to normal.

    - If the dog is conscious, give him warm liquids.

- **Icy Runs**

    - Put kitty litter on the runs or any other place where traction may be difficult for your dog. It will not hurt his feet as conventional rock salt would and is harmless if ingested.

- **Insulated Floors**

    - Cedar shavings will help insulate the floor of your dog's quarters as well as deodorize and deter parasites.

- A dozen thicknesses of newspapers will act as a temporary insulation for a cold floor. Pieces of blanket, rugs, mats, or rags absorb moisture and they must be replaced frequently. It is neither healthy nor comfortable for the dog to lie on a damp surface.

- Electric kennel pads with temperature controls are available in various sizes and may be purchased from pet supply stores. They provide safe, constant warmth for the outdoor doghouse.

- NEVER LET YOUR DOG SLEEP ON BARE STONE OR CONCRETE FLOORS.

- **Metal Water Dish**

  - In freezing weather, metal water dishes should not be used as the dog's warm wet tongue may stick to the metal.

- **Sand**

  - A thin layer of sand on concrete runs eliminates the problem of chipping frozen stools from cement runs during freezing weather. When snow is predicted, add as much as ¼ inch of sand in the kennel. Pens and runs can be cleaned daily for a week before it will be necessary to add more sand to the area.

- **Water Buckets**

  - A plastic pail holds more warmth than a metal one. In a cold climate, the water will not freeze as readily if the plastic bucket is insulated with an inner tube wrapped around it.

- **Winter Freeze**

  - To kill worm eggs and to sweeten the ground, salt and lime down your kennel runs before the winter freeze sets in. Wet the ground, sprinkle salt and lime, and soak again. Dampen intermittently as required to dissolve salt and lime. DO NOT USE FOR THREE DAYS AFTER LIME IS APPLIED.

MEDICATION

Ugh! Where did you get
  That nasty tasting stuff?
Just because I'm off my feed
  You don't have to make it so rough.

SIGNS OF ILLNESS

- Signs of illness in a dog are appetite loss, convulsions, diarrhea, fever, inflammation of the eyes, listlessness, retching, restlessness, and trembling. A hot dry nose does not always indicate illness.

WARNINGS!

- Proper home health care should be a preventive measure not an attempt to provide amateur veterinary treatment.

  - Avoid doctoring with your own prescriptions. Tolerance and overdosage are common dangers.

  - Consult a veterinarian about medication.

  - Many medicines are incompatible so do not mix dosages without your veterinarian's knowledge.

  - Drugs and medications over one year old should not be used. A safe method of disposal is to flush pills and liquid medication down the toilet.

  - If your veterinarian prescribes an antibiotic or any medication, make sure your dog receives ALL the medicine at the correct intervals.

  - Certain drugs can cause some dogs to go into anaphylactic shock. Observe your dog closely after giving him any medication. If he should start coughing, breathing rapidly, sneezing, or swelling, consult a veterinarian immediately.

DOSING

- **Cutting Pills**

  - If a large pill needs to be cut in half, use scissors or large nail trimmers instead of a knife. This prevents crumbling.

- **Disguising Pills**

  - Some dogs take medicine more readily if given with ice cream. To disguise a pill, coat with peanut butter or hamburger.

    Please disguise my medicine
    In something that tastes good
    Otherwise, I won't swallow it,
    Even though I know I should.

  - Try coating the medication with a bit of butter to help it slide down the dog's throat more easily. If butter is placed on the nose first, he will get the taste of the butter and not fight the medicine.

- **Liquid Medicine**

  - Remove the needle from a disposable syringe. Fill with proper dosage of medicine. Release the liquid slowly into the dog's mouth from the side. Especially good for puppies. The syringe may be reused if thoroughly rinsed.

  - For puppies and toy dogs, use an eye dropper.

  - Put the prescribed amount of medication in a small bottle. Pull out the corner of the lower lip to form a pocket. Pour the liquid in small amounts.

  - It is not necessary to open the mouth of the dog to give liquid medicine. Pull out the lower lip and spoon in medication.

- **Storage**

  - Tired of uncapping and capping lids on medicine bottles? Buy a plastic fishing lure box, label each compartment with the name of the medicine and fill with medication.

DRUG DOSAGES

- Any drug is potentially dangerous if the problem is incorrectly diagnosed, if dog is allergic to the medicine, or if medicine is given improperly.

- IF IN DOUBT, CONSULT YOUR VETERINARIAN.

- When administering patient medicine for a common ailment and you do not know the correct dosage, the following is a good rule of thumb. Dose a large dog (100 pounds) the same amount of medication that an average-sized human would take. This rule, however, is to be applied ONLY in an emergency. Dogs, as well as humans, differ so it is wise to consult your veterinarian.

- Before the occasion arises, the authors suggest you take the following list of medication to your veterinarian and have him prescribe the amount of dosage for the size and weight of your particular dog. Write the information in the space provided in this book for future reference.

- **Oral Medication**

    1. **Aspirin**

        Use: Helps relieve pain and reduces fever.

        Dosage: _____

    2. **Charcoal**

        Use: Prevents absorption of toxic material in the body.

        Dosage: _____

    3. **Coca Cola Syrup**

        Use: Helps to control vomiting.

        Dosage: _____

4. **Colace**

   Use: Acts as a stool softener.

   Dosage: _____

5. **Cold Capsules**

   Use: Provides temporary relief of minor nasal and sinus congestion. Do not give for more than two days.

   Dosage: _____

6. **Di-Gel**

   Use: Helps to alleviate gas. May be obtained in either tablet or liquid form.

   Dosage: _____

7. **Dramamine**

   Use: Provides relief for motion sickness. Give at least one hour before starting a trip.

   Dosage: _____

8. **Epsom Salts**

   Use: Is a quick acting cathartic but dogs dislike the bitter taste.

   Dosage: _____

9. **Hydrogen Peroxide (3% Solution)**

   Use: Induces vomiting.

   Dosage: _____

10. **Ipecac Syrup**

   Use: Induces vomiting but is slow acting.

   Dosage: _____

11. **Kaolin-Pectin (Kaopectate)**

   Use: Helps control diarrhea and vomiting.

   Dosage: _____

12. **Milk of Magnesia**

   Use: Works as a laxative as well as an antacid.

   Dosage: _____

13. **Mineral Oil**

   Use: Is a lubricant and a laxative.

   Dosage: _____

14. **Paregoric**

   Use: To ease stomach cramps and diarrhea.

   Dosage: _____

15. **Pepto-Bismol or Bismuth**

   Use: Controls vomiting and diarrhea

   Dosage: _____

16. **Sodium Bicarbonate**

   Use: Is an antacid to control vomiting.

   Dosage: _____

• TOPICAL APPLICATION

1. A & D Ointment

Use: Helps the healing of wounds, soothes irritated skin.

Apply: Rub on irritated skin.

2. BFI Powder

Use: Is an antiseptic and drying powder for minor wounds.

Apply: Use daily on irritated area.

3. Campho-Phenique

Use: Promotes healing of minor cuts and sores. May be obtained as a liquid or salve.

Apply: Use full strength.

4. Chlorine (Clorox)

Use: Irrigates infected wounds. Also good for bacterial or fungal diseases of the skin.

Apply: Mix one-half teaspoon to one cup water. Soak, at least, three times daily.

5. Gentian Violet

Use: Prevents growth of bacteria on skin and promotes healing. Objection is that it is a permanent dye which must wear off.

Apply: Use full strength. May be used frequently. Will not harm dog if licked.

6. Gly-Oxide

Use: Is an antiseptic for the mouth and treatment for minor oral inflammation. Helps destroy bacteria on the teeth.

Apply: Use full strength. Saturate a piece of cotton and wipe teeth and gums several times a week.

7. Hydrogen Peroxide (3% Solution)

Use: Use as an antiseptic and cleanser.

Apply: Use full strength on an affected area.

8. Sodium Bicarbonate

Use: Neutralizes acid burns.

Apply: Mix one tablespoon to one cup of water. Apply and then rinse with clear water.

9. ST-37

Use: Is an antiseptic solution for minor cuts and treatment for ulcers in the mouth.

Apply: For cuts, etc., apply full strength. For the mouth, dilute ST-37 with water 1-1.

10. Vinegar

Use: Neutralizes alkali burns. May also be used for bee stings.

Apply: Use full strength, then rinse with clear water.

• SPECIAL MEDICATION

_____

_____

ADDITIONAL MEDICATON

Recommended by your Veterinarian

R_x————————————————

     Use: ————————————————————

     Dosage: ————————————————————

R_x————————————————

     Use: ————————————————————

     Dosage: ————————————————————

R_x————————————————

     Use: ————————————————————

     Dosage: ————————————————————

R_x————————————————

     Use: ————————————————————

     Dosage: ————————————————————

R_x————————————————

     Use: ————————————————————

     Dosage: ————————————————————

R_x————————————————

     Use: ————————————————————

     Dosage: ————————————————————

NATURAL REMEDIES

*Mother Nature was here
Long before pills.
For thousands of years
She cured our ills.*

Natural Remedies are highly acclaimed by many people.
The authors recommend that good judgment be used in all cases.

IF FACED WITH A LIFE-THREATENING SITUATION, CALL YOUR VETERINARIAN. DO NOT EXPERIMENT IF DANGEROUS SYMPTOMS ARE PRESENT.

ABSCESS

- Sometimes an operation and antibiotics are not successful in getting rid of an abscess. Large doses of multiple vitamins and minerals, plus vitamin C and protein have proven helpful.

- Give garlic internally.

- Use hot fomentation of blackberry or groundsel on the abscess.

- SEE Poultices, page 117.

ANEMIA

- Feed your pet brewer's yeast, boiled eggs, liver, parsley, vegetable greens, vitamin B-12, wheat germ.

ARTHRITIS

- Eliminate acid-type foods.

- Make a tea of alfalfa and pour over food. This is a good body builder and contains more vitamins and minerals than any other plant.

- Mix fresh parsley with the food.

- Massage the afflicted part, three times a day, with the following: four tablespoons of olive oil mixed with one tablespoon of sunflower oil, and ½ teaspoon of eucalyptus oil.

- Put bee pollen on food — one tablespoon, daily, for a medium-sized dog.

BAD BREATH

- Charcoal tablets are helpful if the digestive tract is the problem.

BEE POLLEN

- Through many studies over the last 30 years, bee pollen has been found to be one of the most concentrated and nutritious foods on earth. An excellent scientific study is POLLEN, BIOLOGY, BIOCHEMISTRY, MANAGEMENT by R.G. Stanley and H.F. Linskens, Springer-Verlag, N.Y.

- Bee pollen may be obtained from health food stores.

- Bee pollen can be useful in the following situations:

  - To maintain the good health of a pet. (1 teaspoon per 50 pounds of body weight)

  - Older animals — arthritic. (1 tablespoon daily per 50 pounds of body weight)

  - Pregnant and lactating bitches. (1 tablespoon daily per 50 pounds of body weight)

  - Males at stud. (1 tablespoon daily per 50 pounds of body weight)

  - Show dogs. (1 tablespoon daily per 50 pounds body weight)

  - Animals recovering from injury or sickness (1 tablespoon daily per 50 pounds of body weight)

BEE STING

- Remove the stinger then apply ice until swelling and pain are gone.

- Other natural remedies which may be applied are honey, raw onion, ammonia and water (1-3 mixture), lemon juice or witch hazel.

BLACKSTRAP MOLASSES

- Is an excellent source of calcium and magnesium. Is especially good for in-whelp bitches and growing puppies. Give one tablespoon, daily, for a medium-sized dog.

BLADDER INFECTION

- Females frequently experience bladder infection or vaginitis. One breeder suggests adding a tablespoon of apple cider vinegar per quart of drinking water to clear up such an infection.

- Make a tea of the parsley root and give three times a day.

- Add pure honey to the food.

BONE MEAL

- This natural source of calcium and phosphorus is excellent for puppies and pregnant and lactating bitches. (Dosage: 1 teaspoon for small dogs.) Obtained at health food stores.

BURNS, FIRST DEGREE

- Apply ice water until pain is gone then put on vitamin E.

- Put on ice water until pain diminishes then swab with honey.

- Apply freshly brewed tea.

CONSTIPATION

- Feed dried or fresh fruit and berries.

- Add roughage to the diet.

- Provide more exercise.

- Add liver or milk to the diet.

COUGHING

- Coughing may be a sign of a serious illness. Check with your veterinarian.

*A scratching in my throat
Is keeping me awake.
Do you have something
For my comfort's sake?*

- Pure honey, mixed with lemon, is soothing to the throat.

- If your dog has a slight cough, relieve the condition by putting a dab of butter on his nose. As he licks this, his throat is coated and scarring of the tissue is avoided.

DESSICATED LIVER

- Dessicated liver (dried liver from which fat, tendons, and ligaments have been removed) is an excellent source of Vitamin B Complex.

- Dessicated liver can be bought in tablet or powdered form.

DIARRHEA

- Restrict all food for 24 hours. Give only lemon juice, honey, and garlic.

- Break the fast with small and frequent feedings. Continue for several days.

  - Give boiled rice and/or boiled hamburger which has had all the fat skimmed off.

- Gradually add other bland foods. SEE page 39.

- Do not return to regular food for several days.

- Do not feed your dog any product that contains whey. Whey is the watery part of milk separated from the curd and will cause diarrhea.

DIGESTION

- Sometimes the bacteria in the stomach fails to function properly, especially when dogs have been on a heavy dosage of antibiotics. One tablespoon of buttermilk added to the food daily helps the digestion.

- Yogurt contains lactic acid and helps combat growth of harmful bacteria in the intestines.

EAR CANKER

- Canker of the ear causes a thick black discharge which originates in the lower part of the ear. Open a garlic capsule, press out the juice, and swab the inside of the ear once a day.

- Chronic ear cankers may be caused by a shortage of fat in the diet. A very old treatment is to add bacon fat to the food.

- Cleanse the ear with diluted witch hazel to remove the black discharge so that the air can circulate.

- For drop-eared dogs, shave the inside of the ear or tape them on the top of the head for better air circulation.

EARACHE

- If your dog rubs his ears and appears to have an earache, a drop of warm eucalyptus oil in the ear will help relieve the pain.

EYE INFECTION

- Rosemary is both an antiseptic and a healing herb. Make an infusion of rosemary: 1 cup cold water, 1 teaspoon of dry rosemary, simmer. Let stand for four hours. Bathe eyes twice daily.

- Increase vitamin A by feeding the following: carrots, green leafy vegetables, egg yolk, butter, and cheese.

EYE IRRITATION

- Irritation from dust, smoke, and debris can be treated by applying a drop of castor oil, cod-liver oil, or olive oil into the eye.

EYE STAIN

- Add tomato juice to diet.

- Bathe eyes in camomile, fennel tea, or juice of raw cucumber.

FASTING

- Through the centuries, man has found that fasting helps to regenerate the body. Wild animals did not feed regularly so the body was able to rest from digesting food. If your dog isn't sick but appears lethargic, skip a couple of meals. Give water and honey only. The body has a built-in healing power and the resting of the body helps to eliminate internal toxins.

FEET

- For cracked or sore pads, bathe feet in a strong solution of leaf or pine needle tea.

- Combine kelp, apple-cider vinegar, and warm water and bathe the pads.

- Boil raw potato peelings 15 minutes and soak the dog's pads in water for ten minutes, four times a day.

- SEE Feet, page 57.

FINIKY EATERS

- Brewer's dried yeast (one teaspoon per 25 pounds of dog's weight) encourages the appetite.

FLEAS

- Chemical poisons are probably the most effective way to eliminate fleas. However, there is a danger to you and your pet from these toxic chemicals. Herbal powders, oil, and flea collars may be purchased from health food stores. These products are harmless. They do not kill the fleas but drive them away. However, when the scent dissipates, the problem returns if you do not follow a daily program to eliminate the fleas in the environment.

- Mix with food, one tablespoon of vinegar and increase to four tablespoons each day. It helps clear up fleas. Dogs will have more undercoat and get rid of strange "doggie" odors. (Above dosage is for large dogs.)

- Two garlic capsules given daily has worked for some dog breeders in getting rid of fleas.

- Several tablespoons of baking soda dissolved in a quart of water relieves surface irritation without introducing chemicals into the blood stream or into the open wound.

- Make a lotion of one teaspoonful of eucalyptus oil, two teaspoons of household ammonia, and a half pint of warm water. Apply to the dog's coat.

- A mixture of 50 percent eucalyptus oil and 50 percent water is a good flea repellent. It must be rubbed over the entire dog.

- Brewer's yeast is rich in vitamin B Complex. When metabolized, this releases a sulfurous compound onto the dog's skin. Use one teaspoon per 25 pounds of dog's weight. Besides getting rid of fleas, it gives a nice luster to the coat. Some breeders believe tablets are more successful because of the binder.

- If cedar shavings are used in the dog's bed, fleas will leave as they cannot tolerate the cedar aroma.

- Soak a string or cord in pennyroyal oil and place around your pet's neck. For more protection, mix one teaspoon of pennyroyal with four tablespoons of water and rub on the dog's coat. Do this once a month. It is oily so keep your pet off the carpets. It has a very strong odor.

- Dust doghouse and bedding with salt.

- Use a strong salt solution for washing runs and kennels.

- SEE Fleas, pages 129-131.

FLIES

- To stop flies from annoying the ears of dogs, some breeders add a teaspoon of brewer's yeast daily to the dog's food.

A great place to relax
  Was under an apple tree
But mosquitoes and flies
  Bit the heck out of me.

- A border of marigolds planted near a kennel run, produces an odor which discourages the fly population.

- The leaves from the squash and pumpkin plants are another natural fly repellent.

GARLIC

- Garlic helps to remove the mucus in the intestines.

- If you have no faith in the curative power of garlic or as a flea deterrent, add it anyway to your pet's food for the vitamins, minerals, and roughage.

GAS

- The cure for a "gassy" dog is to give your pet a cup of buttermilk. This would be the dosage for a large dog.

  I know you'll understand
  That I do it because I must
  I try and try to hold it
  But have to let it go or bust.

- In the food, add several cloves of garlic daily.

- If a dog's stomach rumbles, it could be a potassium deficiency. Give him a scraped raw potato. Dandelion greens and black-strap molasses are also rich in potassium.

- Charcoal absorbs toxins in the body.

- Avoid cottage cheese, hard-boiled eggs, excessive meat, too much fat, and vegetables in the cabbage family.

- Yogurt helps restore the good bacteria so the food will digest before it putrefies and causes gas.

HAIR GROWTH

- Add raw chopped dandelion leaves to the food.

- Boil marigold flowers in water and apply liquid to the coat.

- Apply castor oil to the coat. Keep dog off the carpets.

- Add seaweed to the diet. Powder or tablets may be obtained from a health food store.

- Give one tablespoon brewer's yeast, one tablespoon safflower oil, and one vitamin E capsule daily. (Dosage for medium-sized dog.)

- Linoleic acid in the form of safflower or soybean oil is helpful.

HAIR RINSE

- For a gray dog, rinse the coat in sage tea.

- To bring out the highlights and color of a yellow dog, rinse his coat with camomile tea after shampooing.

- To have a sparkling white dog, put several drops of bluing in the shampoo and rinse.

HOT SPOTS

- Usually the treatment needed for hot spots is to change the ph value in the area affected; this can be done by pouring diluted vinegar over the spot.

  You look really worried
  When "hot spots" appear.
  How do you think I feel?
  After all, they're on my rear.

- One breeder reported success in clearing up hot spots with pesticidal shampoo. SEE Pesticidal Shampoo, page 71.

- Puncture and squeeze a vitamin E capsule on hot spot. Vitamin E may also be purchased in liquid form.

- Give vitamin C daily.

HYPER DOG

- Dogs have allergies too. If a medical examination does not reveal why your dog trembles, is "hyper," drinks excessively, and has a loss of appetite, you might suspect an allergy to prepared dog foods which contain preservatives, sugar additives, artificial flavoring, and coloring. Make your own doggy stew. Include beef, brown rice, eggs, vegetables, oatmeal, rye, cornmeal, wheat germ, and brewer's yeast. A large kettle, kept in the refrigerator, is as handy as opening cans.

- For that overactive dog that just won't calm down, try mixing thyme with his food. It is an excellent natural tranquilizer.

- Give vitamins B-1, B-6, and B-15 to the hyper dog.

INDIGESTION

- Give the dog a clove of raw garlic in his food.

- Papaya, containing papain, is used to treat chronic indigestion and chronic diarrhea. You can use papaya in the dog's food or get papain tablets at a health food store. Give one capsule a day for a large dog.

INSECT STINGS

- Fast relief from a wasp or bee sting can be obtained by dabbing the spot with plain vinegar, which neutralizes the acid in the sting. Apply baking soda later.

- Mash a raw onion and apply immediately.

- If nothing else is at hand, make a small mud pie and plaster it over the sting.

KIDNEY AND BLADDER DISORDERS

- This can be a life-threatening situation. Do not experiment if dangerous symptoms are present. If the dog drinks excessively, urinates in increased volume, vomits, lacks appetite and has a weight loss, it is important to take him to the veterinarian immediately.

- Asparagus shoots increase the urine flow and carries ammonia out of the body system.

- Give parsley root tea or add chopped parsley to food.

- Chopped dandelion leaves neutralize uric acid.

- Vitamin C reduces bacteria growth and promotes healing.

LICE

- Take a handful of crushed twigs of the Scotch Broom plant (Cytisus Scoparius) and boil in olive oil. Apply this solution to the dog's coat.

- An excellent remedy for external parasites is to brew one handful of Scotch Broom tops in one quart of water and apply to coat.

MINERALS

- SEE Appendix for CHART ON MINERALS.

MOSQUITO REPELLENT

- Mosquitoes frequently attack the head and the legs of a dog. Mix two cups of warm water with two drops of eucalyptus oil and rub on the dog. Avoid getting in the eyes. Very strong odor.

Try a few things that have worked
With some of my friends.
Anything at all—
Just so the itching ends.

- Certain mosquitoes cause heartworm in dogs. Eliminate mosquito breeding areas and use mosquito repellents.

- The distilled oil of the pennyroyal plant is a powerful mosquito repellent.

- Basil planted near the dog area helps discourage mosquitoes and flies.

MOUTH SORES

- Give, daily, niacin (B-3), riboflavin (B-2), and vitamin A.

- Paint with gentian violet.

- Give vitamin C, daily.

- A weak salt solution rubbed onto the gums two or three times a week helps prevent pyorrhea associated with tartar build up.

- Several times a day apply diluted Hydrogen Peroxide.

MUCUS-FREE DIET

- Eliminate fats, milk, and milk products. Feed fruits, nuts, and green leafy vegetables.

- Cloves of garlic added to the food is helpful in eliminating mucus in the stool.

NUTRIENTS FOR SICKLY PUPPIES

- Grate several almond kernels and mix with milk. Give one teaspoon of grated almonds twice a day.

- One teaspoon of honey, daily, is helpful.

- Give the puppy whole goats' milk.

POULTICES

- Poultices have been used since ancient times for drawing toxins from the skin, reducing inflammation, and curing sores.

- Spread a boiled turnip on a bandage and apply to sore.

- Mix onion with honey or olive oil and apply to inflamed area.

- Heat ½ raw onion over flame and apply to sore. Bandage lightly.

- Apply a poultice of fresh comfrey leaves.

RINGWORM

- Mix mild ivory soap and garlic juice. Apply and leave on overnight. Rinse in the morning.

- Apply vitamin E to the spot for two weeks.

SALIVA (EXCESSIVE)

- If excessive salivation is not normal for your dog, check his mouth for bad teeth, cuts, etc.

- Excessive salivation may be a phosphorus deficiency. Feed your dog cottage cheese, egg yolk, green vegetables, and beef.

SCARRING, LESS

- Vitamin E oil used on cuts and scratches helps to prevent the formation of scar tissue.

SHAMPOO (DRY)

- Rub cornmeal into the coat. Comb and brush out. Repeat several times for best results.

SKIN PROBLEMS

- If your dog has skin problems, avoid foods that contain any form of soybeans. Soybeans cause a depletion of zinc in the body. Zinc is very healing and is frequently used in ointments.

Intelligent I am
But I cannot read.
So aid from you
Is what I need.

- To help clear up a dog's eczema, mix with the food two tablespoons of cottage cheese, two tablespoons of corn oil, six drops of vitamin E, and one capsule of garlic.

- Zinc deficiency is often characterized by skin lesions.

- Almond oil is an excellent external remedy for sores.

- To prevent hot spots or summer eczema, cut down on fats such as bacon grease, lamb fat, or suet.

- The flowers of the Scotch Broom shrub, steeped in hot milk, help to heal certain forms of skin ailments.

- To clear up some skin problems, combine the bruised leaves of chickweed with olive oil, let stand overnight, and apply.

- Pantothenic Acid, vitamin B, and vitamin C are most helpful to the skin.

SLUG BAIT

- A harmless method for killing slugs is to place several pans containing beer in the yard. Slugs attracted by the odor will drown.

SNAKEBITE

- Until it is possible to give anti-venin shot, give your dog massive dosage of vitamin C.

SOLAR DERMATITIS

- Powdered seaweed and vitamin C added to the dog's food help to darken the nose if solar dermatitis is the problem.

- Keep dog out of direct sunlight.

SOYMILK

- Soymilk is an excellent protein supplement as it contains iron and many B vitamins. May be purchased in health food stores.

SPIDER BITES

- Apply a mixture of salt, soda, and water to the bite.

SPRAINS

- Comfrey poultices are helpful for swellings and sprains.

- Confine the dog as much as possible.

- During the first few hours after an injury, apply cold compresses every fifteen minutes.

SPROUTS

- Sprouts make a healthful and inexpensive addition to the dog's food. You may use the whole grain of alfalfa, oats, rye, wheat, etc. or whole, unhulled seeds such as dried beans or sunflower seeds. Besides cutting down on food bills, sprouts provide valuable vitamins and minerals.

STOMACH UPSET

- Mix equal amounts of sauerkraut juice and tomato juice. Give one teaspoon every hour.

SUNLIGHT

- Sunlight is important to your dog's health. It is an excellent source of vitamin D which is needed for growth, strong bones, and teeth.

- The body's nervous system is helped by sunlight.

- Except for solar dermatitis, sunlight is an aid to most skin disorders.

- Too much sunlight can dry out a dog's coat.

TAPEWORM

- To remove the last ribbon of a tapeworm, give the equivalent of eight ounces of pumpkin seed. (Dosage is for large dog.)

URINARY ACIDIFIERS

- Tomato juice and cranberry juice are excellent urinary acidifiers.

VITAMINS

- SEE Appendix for CHART ON VITAMINS.

VOMITING (Emetic)

- Vomiting from eating couch grass should not be discouraged as it is a natural way to cleanse the stomach. If necessary, plant a small patch in your yard. Some apartment dwellers keep a flower pot or two of this grass for the dog's sole use.

WARTS

- Apply liquid vitamin E (stick a pin in a capsule and squeeze out or buy liquid form) on the wart twice a day. The wart should dry up in about a week.

WATER RETENTION

- Parsley contains a great deal of potassium which combats water retention and bloat.

WORMS

- One dog owner claims that a pinch of tobacco is a sure cure for eradication of some types of worms.

WOUNDS

- Allow the dog to lick minor wound, especially if there is pus.

For ages and ages
We learned to survive.
We depended upon Nature
To keep us alive.

- If wound becomes irritated from constant licking, it may be necessary to use an Elizabethan collar. SEE Bandage or Wound Protection, page 47.

- Bathe wound with a solution of rosemary made in the following manner: add two cups of water to one cup of fresh rosemary. Boil for three minutes. Allow to steep overnight in a glass jar.

- A wound that the dog cannot reach to lick should be bandaged to keep out of the dirt.

The authors do not recommend the use of herbs as a form of treatment for sickness without veterinarian approval. Certainly when serious symptoms are present, a veterinarian should be consulted.

ADDITIONAL NATURAL REMEDIES

Recommended by Friends

N_R——————————

    Use: _____

    Dosage: _____

N_R——————————

    Use: _____

    Dosage: _____

N_R——————————

    Use: _____

    Dosage: _____

N_R——————————

    Use: _____

    Dosage: _____

N_R——————————

    Use: _____

    Dosage: _____

N_R——————————

    Use: _____

    Dosage: _____

N_R——————————

    Use: _____

    Dosage: _____

OLDER DOG

My fur is thinning
My muzzle is gray.
Sometimes I think
I've had my day.

INDICATIONS

- Cataracts
- Chronic coughs
- Coat is dull and thin
- Deafness
- Graying (this can happen in younger dogs)
- Loose teeth with excessive tartar
- Loss of bladder control
- Obesity
- Partial paralysis
- Sleeps more
- Stiff limbs
- Tumor formations
- Warts
- Watery eyes

TIPS FOR COMFORT

- Avoid too much exercise
- Avoid drafts
- Carry upstairs if necessary
- Clean ears regularly
- Eliminate stress
- Follow established routines
- Groom regularly
- If blind, walk on leash
- Keep free from parasites
- Keep teeth free from tartar
- Massage stiff legs
- Provide softer and warmer beds
- Thoroughly dry after exposure to rain or snow.

AGE OF DOG COMPARED WITH MAN

Dog Years	Man Years	Dog Years	Man Years
1	15	9	52
2	24	10	56
3	28	11	60
4	32	12	64
5	36	13	68
6	40	14	72
7	44	15	76
8	48	16	80

ARTHRITIS

- Inflamation of the joints is painful to the dog and he doesn't want to move. Exercise is good for those old aching legs; otherwise, he will just get stiffer and be in more pain. Exercise, of course, should be moderate.

- Waterbeds are helpful for arthritic and rheumatic dogs. They are non-allergenic and easily cleaned. May be obtained at many leading pet supply stores.

- SEE Arthritis, page 105.

BLINDNESS

- As dog's sight dims, his other senses quicken.

- Keep food and water dishes in same spot.

- Don't leave the dog outside alone.

My vision no longer
Is quite so keen
I frequently act
Crochety and mean.

- Exercise your dog on a leash.

- Pet and speak to him frequently...it gives him a sense of security.

- Keep area clear of unfamiliar objects.

DEAFNESS

- Old, deaf dogs can, to a certain extent, "hear" through vibrations.

- Poor hearing can often be improved by proper treatment and care. Ear mites, foreign material, or accumulation of ear wax, can cause pain and loss of hearing.

- Senility can cause loss of hearing or deafness.

- Communication will be easier between your old, deaf dog and you if you have taught him hand signals for "Come," "Sit," "Stand," "Stay," etc. before he loses his hearing.

DRINKING

- Older dogs will drink more but excessive drinking may indicate trouble. Report such changes to your veterinarian.

EARS

- Head shaking and scratching of the ear may indicate external ear infection. Better check with your veterinarian.

- Clean ears by putting in a few drops of mineral oil. Massage and then remove the excess oil with cotton.

EXERCISE

- Older dog's exercise periods should be short.

EYES

- There may be discharge and weeping of the eyes. Soothe the eyes by bathing with water, herbal solutions, boric acid, or commercial preparations.

- A cataract is the clouding of part or all of the lens. Operations may be performed by a specialist. The operation will not be completely successful but your pet may regain part of his sight.

GROOMING

- The skin of older dogs is drier so limit the number of baths and substitute frequent brushing.

NAILS

- Trim nails regularly. The aging dog is exercising less and is not wearing his nails down.

- SEE Dry Nails, page 81.

NATURAL DEATH

- A dog's life is all too short. Unless he is in pain, let him die a natural death. It will cause you more work and problems but it is your way of thanking him for the unselfish love he has given you through the years.

Don't feel so bad.
We've had it good...
You've made me happier
Than anyone could!

NEW DOG

- The sooner you get a new puppy after the death of your older pet, the better. In no way does it diminish the love you have for the old one; actually, it is a tribute to his memory.

- If your old pet is an only dog, wait until he is gone before introducing a new one into the family.

NUTRITION AND DIET

- Older dogs exercise less so their caloric intake should be less.

- Prescription diets may be necessary for cardiac and kidney diseases. Ask your veterinarian.

- If you have been using a good dog food, continue to do so but decrease the amount of calories up to 20 percent. Supplement your dog's food with vitamins and minerals. Check with your veterinarian.

- Cut down on starchy foods. Don't eliminate them entirely but replace a portion with carrots, green beans, and other vegetables.

  I'm a senior citizen
  And have to take it easy...
  A little different food
  And my stomach gets queasy.

- Veal is exceptionally good for the senior citizen or one suffering from kidney problems.

- Divide the allotted food rations into two parts. Feed ½ in the morning and ½ in the evening.

- Add parsley and dandelions to the diet for additional vitamins and minerals.

- If the teeth are bad, soften the food with warm water.

- SEE Special Diets, page 39.

- Fat puts strain on the body. Obesity makes corrective surgery more dangerous and your pet will be more prone to illnesses such as diabetes and heart trouble.

STRESS

- Serve meals at the same time and at the same place.

- Provide exercise on a regular schedule.

- Protect your senior citizen from stressful situations, such as: firecrackers, excitable children, new puppies, etc.

- Special care should be given to your pet when moving to a new area.

- Do not give a new dog more attention than you give the old one.

TEETH

- Scaling teeth will help prevent periodontal disease.

- Remove any diseased teeth.

- Brush teeth with a salt and soda solution.

- Chew bones and dog biscuits help remove stains and tartar.

TEMPERATURE SENSITIVITY

- Old dogs are sensitive to temperature extremes. They get chilled or overheated easily.

Often times my back legs
Give me much pain...
Rheumatiz perhaps
From the cold and rain.

- In extremely hot weather, keep your dog indoors and as cool as possible. Feed lightly and sponge off frequently.

- In cold weather, dry your dog thoroughly if he has been out in the snow or rain. A sweater may be practical for some dogs.

URINARY STONES

- Frequently stones form in older dogs. If they form in the kidneys, it may cause nephritis. The formation in the bladder may lead to chronic cystitis.

- The dog will be in pain and will attempt to urinate with little or no success.

- X-ray is the only sure way of determining if there are stones.

URINE DRIBBLING

- Older spayed females may dribble urine. Check bedding. This is not serious unless there is an urinary disease so check with your veterinarian. This problem can be controlled by hormone tablets.

PARASITES

*Drat those !☆ *!# fleas;*
  They're biting my ears and tail.
You just have to find relief for me...
  Please do it without fail.

EXTERNAL PARASITES

DANGERS FROM FLEAS

- Cause severe allergic reaction in some dogs.
- May carry tapeworm to your dog.
- Spread and intensify summer skin disease.
- Scratching may cause serious skin infection.

FACTS ABOUT FLEAS

- Fleas do not reproduce themselves on the dog.
- Flea eggs are white and about the size of a grain of salt.
- Eggs drop off the dog into crevices, bedding, furniture, etc.
- Moisture and heat are essential for hatching.
- Eggs hatch into larvae. They are about one-fourth inch long, white to creamy.
- The dark gritty particles found on the dog are deposits of flea excrement.
- One female may lay 500 eggs in her lifetime of 200 days.
- Fleas hop from one dog to another.

FLEA CONTROL

- Chemical remedies to be found in pet supply stores, pharmacies, veterinary clinics, supermarkets, include:

  - Collars
  - Insecticidal Dips
  - Oral medication
  - Pendants

- Powders
- Soaps
- Sprays
- Sticks

I look all spruce and clean
But am not at all at ease
I have to scratch constantly
And my problems could be fleas.

- **Treatment of Premises**

  - Fumigate with insecticides
  - Use flea bomb or fogger
  - Vacuum often...burn contents of bag
  - Wash or burn infected bedding

ALWAYS FOLLOW INSTRUCTIONS EXPLICITLY WHEN USING FLEA BOMBS OR INSECTICIDES!

FLEA TIPS FROM BREEDERS AND DOG OWNERS

- **Breath of Pine.** Is an inexpensive way to deodorize and repel fleas and ticks on your dog. Pour a tablespoon of this household disinfectant in a spray bottle and fill with water.

- **Calamine or "Caladryl" Lotion.** Is an excellent relief for flea allergy or insect bites. Use Calamine as a lotion after dog has had a medicated bath. When dried it forms a protective cover on the flea bites. Dogs find it distasteful to lick.

- **Flea Dip Procedure**

  - Wear rubber gloves while working on the dog.

  - Put vaseline over your dog's eyelids and around his eyes.

  - The scrotum of male dogs should be covered with vaseline.

  - Soak the dog with clear water before using flea dip.

  - Do not keep old dip that has been mixed.

  - Apply the dip and allow to dry naturally without toweling.

  - Do not let small children play with the dog until he is dry. Even then, the residue of the pesticide might be harmful.

- **Flea Powder.** Select a flea powder with a pyrethrum base. This powder is not toxic to your dog.

  Something's crawling on me;
  That I certainly know.
  Look me over carefully
  And you'll find it's so!

- **Oral Medication.** There is an oral medication containing an insecticide on the market which is absorbed into the bloodstream. When the flea ingests the dog's blood, it dies within three hours. It is registered with the FDA and may be obtained from a veterinarian only.

- **Pine Oil.** One part Pine Oil to 80 parts of water is excellent in repelling fleas. Use in the dog's bath and to disinfect your dog's quarters.

- SEE Fleas, page 111.

LICE

- Serious infestations of lice may cause anemia.

- Control of lice is merely CLEANLINESS.

- Lice are spread by direct contact. Do not use the same grooming equipment on different dogs.

- Lice cause intense itching and can also carry certain tapeworm larvae.

- Pine oil solution used for fleas and ticks will kill lice.

- Comb your dog with a fine-tooth comb to remove the eggs. Place him on a newspaper when you comb and burn the paper immediately.

- Many insecticides will kill lice but most will not kill nits (lice eggs). In heavily infested dogs, it may be necessary to clip all the hair. Follow this with a flea and tick dip every ten days to break the cycle of reproduction.

- Most products for tick and flea control will also kill lice. Check manufacturer's claims.

TICKS

- **Dangers from Ticks**

  - Anemia due to blood loss

  - Paralysis

  - Dermatitis

  - Protozoan blood infection

  - Rocky Mountain Spotted Fever (from wood ticks)

- **Prevention**

  - If you live in a tick-infested area, inspect your dog daily.

  - Keep weeds and underbrush cut closely. If possible, burn the underbrush.

    A bug that makes me miserable
    Is the little gray tick.
    You might become suspicious
    If you see me scratch and lick.

  - Tick and flea dips or sprays will kill ticks in four or five days.

  - An adult tick can lay approximately 5000 eggs so just one tick in the house can call for emergency measures. Either have commercial exterminators fumigate your house or spray insecticides in cracks and crevices.

  - A tick-infested area may be sprayed with four tablespoons of nicotine sulphate (40 percent nicotine) to three gallons of water. If you want more permanent results and do not care about the vegetation, add 4 ounces of sodium fluoride to the above mixture. Both of these ingredients ARE POISONOUS TO DOGS. Use with care.

  - The bed, bedding, and quarters of tick-infested dogs must be thoroughly cleaned and disinfected until all traces of the pest have disappeared.

- **Tick Paralysis**

  - Only a small percentage of tick bites causes paralysis. However, a pregnant female tick could cause your dog to lose coordination, run into things, stagger, and hind legs can collapse without warning. There is usually partial or total recovery in 12 hours after removal of the tick.

  - Male ticks do not swell after ingesting blood from a dog and do not cause paralysis.

- **Tick Removal**

  - Coat tick with petroleum jelly, salad oil, or anything to close the tick's respiratory apparatus. It will release its grip.

  - Drench the tick with rubbing alcohol or camphor. This numbs the tick and makes for easier removal.

  - Use tweezers to remove the tick. The entire tick *must* be removed or the imbedded head may cause an infection or cyst.

  - A drop of turpentine or nail polish remover **on** the tick will cause it to release its hold.

  - When a tick is swollen, tie a slipknot in a piece of strong thread, slip over tick, pull noose close to dog's skin. A quick pull tightens the knot and out pops the tick intact.

  - Always burn or crush the ticks after removal or they may lay eggs and start an infestation.

  - After removal of a tick, apply hydrogen peroxide or another antiseptic for a few days.

  - Do not crush ticks between fingers as this may transfer disease organisms.

- **Warning**

  - Do not mix pesticides by using both a dip and a flea soap. USE ONE OR THE OTHER...NOT BOTH!

INTERNAL PARASITES

PERTINENT INFORMATION

- No one drug can kill all parasites.

- Microscopic fecal examination by a trained technician is the ONLY way to arrive at a proper diagnosis.

These tiny, tiny parasites
That gnaw at my insides
Make me do strange things
And this can be your guide.

- DO NOT DIP AND WORM DOG ON THE SAME DAY.

- Picking up dog stools may not eliminate parasites but does keep the problem at a minimum so the dog does not reinfect himself.

- Remove flea collar before worming dog and leave off for five days. Your veterinarian should be informed about dog having used a flea collar recently.

- **Four Common Varieties are:**

  - Hookworms.
  - Roundworms.
  - Tapeworms.
  - Whipworms.

- **How Dogs Get Worms:**

  - Ingestion.
  - Insect bites.
  - Intermediate host.
  - Prenatal infection.

- It is NOT ADVISABLE to worm a dog yourself UNLESS you

  1. Can evaluate the condition of the dog.
  2. Have a good knowledge of the drugs to be used.
  3. Know correct amount of worm remedy.
  4. Understand the parasite's life cycle.

HEARTWORM

- These parasites depend upon insects for transmission. Heartworm inhabits the great vein, the right side of the heart, and the pulmonary arteries.

- **Symptoms**

  - Tires easily.

  - Has chronic cough.

  - Breathes with difficulty.

  - Has weight loss.

- **Detection**

  - The only way to determine heartworm is by a microscopic examination of the blood.

- **Treatment**

  - Surgery or drugs.

- **Prevention**

  - Check dogs every six months for infection if you live in an endemic area.

  - Control mosquitoes.

- **Control Program**

  - After a blood test determines the dog is free of heartworm, a veterinarian can give prophylactic medication during the mosquito season.

  - There are a number of fly and mosquito repellents made for horses that are excellent for dogs.

- Martins eat millions of mosquitoes every day. Erect several Martin bird houses on your property.

HOOKWORM

- HOOKWORM CANNOT BE DIAGNOSED AND TREATED EFFECTIVELY WITHOUT YOUR VETERINARIAN'S HELP.

- **Description**

  - Hookworms are one-fourth to one-half inch long. They have a reddish or grayish hue.

  - They attach to the wall of small intestine and suck blood.

- **Symptoms**

  - Hookworm larvae migrating through the skin can cause itching.

  - Hookworm in the intestines can cause blood-streaked diarrhea, pale gums, weight loss, weakness, mucous stools (in severe cases black, tarry stools).

- **Control**

  - Hookworm eggs can be destroyed in a kennel run by mixing five gallons of water with 15 pounds of salt. This will cover 500 square feet. Apply once a month.

    CAUTION: Use in a kennel run only as salt will kill vegetation.

  - A concentrated borax (sodium borate) solution may be used instead of salt. Will not kill vegetation.

ROUNDWORMS

- **Description**

  - Whitish or yellowish in color.

  - Approximately five inches long.

  - Pointed at each end.

  - Curled up when alive.

  - Straightened out when dead.

- **Symptoms**

  - Puppy is pot-bellied yet unthrifty in appearance.

  - Gums are anemic.

  - Diarrhea is present.

  - Occasional vomiting.

  - Worms in stool.

- **Detection**

  - Stool sample analysis.

  - Observation.

- **Prevention**

  - Worm eggs can be destroyed by mixing one gallon of water with 2¾ pounds of table salt and applying to kennel runs at the rate of one gallon to 100 sq. ft. of run. Apply once a month.

  - Keep stools picked up and wash the dog's bedding frequently to prevent reinfestation.

- Borax is helpful in controlling round and whipworm eggs and doesn't kill the grass. Use a lawn spreader for large areas.

TAPEWORMS

- Tapeworms are intestinal parasites. At one stage of their life, they pass through an intermediate host (flea, rodent, infected fish, raw pork, or beef).

- **Description**

  - Fresh segments are opaque white or pinkish white, flat, and somewhat rectangular in shape.

  - Dried segments are yellowish and shaped like grains or rice.

- **Prevention**

  - Eliminate fleas and rodents and inspect raw meat carefully.

- **Symptoms**

  - Mild diarrhea.

  - Scratching at the anus.

  - Hearty appetite with no weight gain.

  To me it's not very funny
  * When I'm sliding on my rear—*
  Better take me to the vet;
  * It could be worms, I fear.*

  - Small segments of tapeworm may be found in the stool, in hair around the anus, or in the bedding.

WHIPWORM

- Whipworms are intestinal parasites living in the large intestines. They are about as thick as a coarse thread. Three-quarters of length is hairlike; the last quarter is thicker.

- Many of the same symptoms of hookworm infection.

- Eggs need a wet environment. Keep dog's quarters dry.

PROBLEMS

When I'm very little
* You ought to know...*
That when I gotta go,
* I gotta go!*

ANAL GLANDS

- If a dog isn't sitting straight or seems uncomfortable while sitting, have a veterinarian check his anal glands. Impacted and/or infected anal glands can cause enough discomfort to make the dog prefer to stand.

- Inflammation of the anal glands can be caused by constipation, injury, or blocking of the opening.

BAD BREATH—COMMON CAUSES

- Loose, rotting teeth

- Tartar on teeth

- Pyorrhea

- Ulcerative stomatitis (check for gray ulcers on inside of mouth)

- Tonsillitis

- Advanced case of kidney disease may cause the breath to have a urine-like odor

- Stomach disorder

BARKING DOGS

- A barking dog that keeps the neighbors awake at night should be fed late in the evening so he will be drowsy and sleep through most of the night.

- A barking dog is often a bored dog.

To bark or not to bark
O what the hell...
Sometimes you praise me
Sometimes you yell.

- Excessive barking can be stopped instantly with the use of an electronic shock collar. Inquire at a pet supply store for particulars. Dog magazines often have ads for this product. The use of this product depends on the dog's temperament.

- Some dogs will bark at night. To eliminate shouting at the dogs, install an electric light in their quarters and a switch by your bed. If barking starts, switch light on and off. This will generally stop the barking.

- If your dog continues to bark after you have reprimanded him, investigate the cause. A dog's hearing is so much keener than yours, and he is more aware when things are amiss.

- An intercom between kennel and house provides a means of quieting the barking dog. It also gives peace of mind and alerts you to unusual happenings in the kennel.

- If your barking dog annoys neighbors, you might consider a minor operation for debarking. Check with your veterinarian.

- Buy a Basenji — the no-barking dog!

- SEE Barking Dogs, page 181

BITERS

- An aggressive, overactive puppy should not be played with in a rough and tumble fashion; otherwise, the playful nipping could develop into a problem biter.

- Keeping your dog away from family groups when visitors arrive will build up animosity toward strangers. If the dog is incorrigible at first, put him on a leash and tie to a table leg until he quiets down.

- Do not show approval in an overprotective dog.

- Never allow your puppy to have physical mouth contact while playing or it may result in biting under stress later in life.

  He was trying to take my bone...
  That's why I bit him.
  Teeth are my only weapons.
  I couldn't very well hit him.

- Obedience training is effective if instructor is trained to work with problem dogs.

- Do not keep the dog under constant confinement behind fences or on tether without socialization. Social isolation triggers territorial defense. Bring visitors into his area while he is still a puppy.

- There is usually a reason for biting so try to find the cause.

- Castration may be an answer.

CHASING CARS

- A battery operated device which sends out high-frequency sound waves is a humane method of correcting car chasing because there are not lasting, harmful effects. Information on this device can be found at pet supply stores.

- A safe but uncomfortable device to discourage dogs from chasing cars, is a broom handle cut the width of the dog. Bore a hole through the center, run a

  Chasing cars
  Is a lot of fun,
  They go even faster
  Than I can run.

  cord through, and knot the end. Tie the other end to the dog's collar so length reaches his knees. There will be no trouble walking but in running, the stick gets between the legs.

- DOG-STOPPER is an effective product for car chasers and fighters. It has been tested and approved by the U.S. Department of Agriculture, humane societies, and veterinarians. The product is an aerosol foam which attacks all the dog's senses simultaneously but has no harmful physiological effects. SEE Chasing Cars, page 184.

CHEWERS

- Destructive chewing may be due to teething, boredom, mineral deficiency, or frustration. Tabasco Sauce on tempting objects is effective against chewing.

- Oil of citronella is very unpleasant tasting and discourages chewing.

- Inactivity can result in chewing. Exercise your dog more.

- If your dog chews furniture legs, apply oil of cloves — the bitter taste discourages him.

- Bitter Apple (spray or liquid form) applied to furniture is a harmless and effective deterrent. It may be purchased at pet supply stores.

- If a dog is left alone for long periods, the noise in the environment such as bulldozing, hammering, door bells, telephones, etc. may make him nervous, and he will take out his frustrations on your furniture.

- Substitute rawhide chew bones for valuable furniture.

- If a mature dog destroys property in the house when left alone, try turning on the radio or TV when you leave.

- Pretend you are leaving the house but slip back and catch him in the act and punish severely.

- Wrap a big knuckle bone in many layers of newspapers. Use tape instead of string to hold it together. He will spend much time getting to his prize and the rest of the time chewing on it. (Bones are greasy so the dog should not have access to carpeted areas.)

- If all else fails, crate him.

COPROPHAGY (STOOL EATING)

- Clean the runs and remove stools frequently.

- See that your dog is getting sufficient cereal in his diet so his craving for carbohydrates will be appeased.

- Some breeders have successfully used a self-feeding dry dog food program to correct this disgusting habit.

- Add a generous tablespoon of vinegar to food each day. (Dosage for medium-sized dog.)

- Add the enzyme PAPAIN to the food. This can be obtained by sprinkling ACCENT or ADOLPH'S MEAT TENDERIZER in the dog's food.

- If all else fails, ask the veterinarian for butyric acid capsules. These will give the stools a very unpleasant taste.

- Put red pepper or Tabasco Sauce on stools. A few times of this and your dog should lose interest!

- Pour kerosene on the stools. This will kill grass.

DIGGERS

- Set several mouse traps in his digging area. They will not hurt the dog but the noise will often frighten and surprise him.

As a No, No
It looms big...
But, how I love
To get out and dig!

- Partially fill the hole with dog droppings, then cover the hole with dirt.

- Red pepper sprinkled on the area where the dog likes to dig often discourages the habit. A few drops of pennyroyal oil or citronella is also a deterrent.

- Discourage digging in a likely spot by placing chicken wire just below the surface and cover with a thin layer of soil.

- If neighborhood dogs leave unwanted presents in your yard, bury a number of beer bottles filled with ammonia. The dogs will avoid your yard like the plague until the ammonia evaporates.

DOG FIGHTS

- A good way to break up a dog or cat fight is to douse the combatants with cold water. A hose or a bucket of water is usually sufficient.

- A water pistol may not be sufficient to break up a fight, but in the preliminary stages it often prevents one from starting. Direct the stream of water to the face.

- A chemical "gun" such as carried by meter readers and mailmen contains non-hazardous material that will incapacitate the fighter. Check local police for legalization of this device.

- Avoid areas where ill-tempered dogs reign supreme.

- Muzzle aggressive dogs and keep them together night and day except at mealtime. It may take two weeks to overcome their desire to fight but the effort is worth it.

- If a small dog is attacked by a large one, do not pick up the smaller dog. Grab the hind legs of the attacker which will put him off balance and the little one will be able to run away. If the large dog turns on you, steer him as a wheelbarrow. If he becomes unmanageable, throw him as hard as you can and yell. Hopefully, the anger in your voice and the rough treatment will discourage him. This is a very dangerous procedure. Before you attempt this, know your own capabilities in handling such a situation.

- Do not grab the collars of the fighters or they may turn on you.

- It isn't easy but keep calm. Your shouting may be interpreted by your dog as a cheering section and will only spur him on.

- Hitting a dog with a stick often excites him more.

- From the very first, let your dog know you will not tolerate fighting. Firm correction is preferable to serious injury.

DOG PACKS

- Even a well-trained, obedient pet, if allowed to run free with no supervision, may join other dogs. These packs cause much destruction and fear and have been known to even kill. Your dog is YOUR responsibility.

DOGS ON FURNITURE

- If your dog jumps on the varnished surface of a chair and leaves tell-tale scratches, don't despair. Apply clear transparent plastic contact paper such as used for shelves. The heat of your body will eventually cause the plastic to take on the appearance of the original surface and protect wood from future scratches.

- To prevent his dog from jumping on the furniture to look out the window, an enterprising man removed a small piece of siding at floor level and installed the dog's own window to view the outside world.

- Cover the furniture with a piece of plastic. Under the plastic, set a mouse trap. The noise, plus the uncomfortable plastic, will discourage the dog in short order.

FOURTH OF JULY — LOUD NOISES

- Be sympathetic, but not overly so or you will have an even greater problem to correct.

- Put the dog in a room with the radio turned on.

- If dog is greatly upset, do not feed.

- Keep dog confined or tied. The instinct for self preservation will cause him to run to escape the noise and he may become lost.

- The hearing of a dog is 40 percent more acute than that of a human. Perhaps a piece of cotton in his ears might help deaden loud noises.

- If only one of your dogs is frightened by loud noises, keep him isolated or all of them will try to get in the act.

- Fireworks, loud noises, thunderstorms, etc. may greatly frighten a dog. Give him a sedative prescribed by your veterinarian.

GARBAGE CAN TIPPERS

- Take an old rag and secure it on the lid of the garbage can and soak with household ammonia.

- Sprinkle the top layer of the garbage can with cayenne pepper or ammonia.

- String together a number of tin cans and fasten to the handle of the garbage can. The noise will usually discourage your dog.

INTRODUCING ANOTHER DOG

- Some animals are very anti-social and possessive. Trouble may result if two such animals are put together. Keep the two animals in separate rooms for several days. Then change rooms so they will become familiar with each other's scents. Do this for a couple of weeks before putting them together.

- Take dogs to neutral territory to get acquainted. Keep leads on both dogs until they accept each other.

- One dog will be dominant — let them work it out.

- Dogs adjust easier to each other if they have been neutered or are not of the same sex.

LOST DOG

- Dogs can get lost easily after a snow as familiar scents are covered up. Keep your dog on a leash when exercising.

- Moving into a new area is stressful for dogs until they get used to unfamiliar sights and smells. They may even try to find their old home. Keep dogs tied until they adjust to the new area.

- Tatooing is a protection against dognappers and helps in recovering lost dogs. For a small fee, you can register your name, address, and Social Security Number with one of two national organizations. Your number is then tatooed on the dog's inner right hind leg by a veterinarian. The Registry does not tatoo the dog. Applicatons may be obtained from: National Dog Registry, 227 Stebbin Road, Carmel, New York 10512; or Ident-a-Pet, 401 Broadhollow Road, Melville, New York 11746.

- **Organize Your Search**

  - Most dogs are found within a 10-mile radius of place last seen. The following methods have been successful in finding lost dogs:

    - Contact principals of schools to ask teachers to relay information to students.

    - Alert every veterinary hospital in the area, especially if your dog has a chronic ailment.

    - Give description of dog to local radio station.

- Place ads in newspapers.

- Canvas neighborhood.

- Check with humane society.

- Contact mail carriers.

- Check school bus drivers.

- Talk to the milkman.

- Contact the state veterinarian society and have them relay your loss through a newsletter to all veterinarians.

- Alert all law enforcement agencies: police, sheriff, and state patrol.

- Contact the CB fraternity in your area.

- Post notices and rewards in stores, Laundromat, and on public bulletin boards. A picture is always helpful.

- Contact the State Game and Fish Commission if you last saw your dog in a wilderness area.

- Send fliers to every post-office box in your area.

- Leave crate and dish of food in area where dog was last seen. In the crate leave an article of clothing with your scent on it.

- If dog was tatooed, check with the National Registry or Ident-a-Pet Organization.

- Check with breed clubs in your area.

- Contact youth organizations in your community, such as 4-H Club, Girl Scouts, Boy Scouts, Campfire Girls, etc.

- Don't give up. Sometimes it takes weeks to locate your pet.

NERVOUS DOG

- Dogs that are nervous, full of irrational fears and anxiety, should be reassured and the cause removed. If this doesn't work, don't ignore the distress but see your veterinarian. It may be a medical problem.

- Dogs are sensitive. If you are very upset, your tensions will be felt by your dog. Put him in another room or outdoors until you calm down.

    I don't read the papers
    And seldom watch TV.
    You do...and get upset
    And the tension gets to me.

- More exposure to the public is helpful. Visit shopping centers, busy streets, playgrounds, and parks.

- Enroll in an obedience class. Select an instructor who is knowledgeable and understands your particular problem. The socialization with other dogs and people should prove beneficial.

PILFERING PUPS

- If you have a large puppy that can reach the top of the kitchen counter, you can protect food by opening the drawer under the counter top and blocking the drawer open. The pup is too far away to plunder.

POISON IVY

- Do not pet your dog if he has been romping in an area where there is poison ivy. The poison ivy on a dog's coat will not bother him, but the residue may get on your skin. Put on rubber gloves before handling. Rinse your dog in salt water and follow with a clear water rinse.

REPELLENTS

- Apply repellent to furniture or garden while disciplining the dog for destructive behavior such as wetting, digging, scratching, etc. The odor of the repellent lingers and reminds him of the scolding.

- If male dogs are a problem when your bitch is in heat, purchase a protective non-staining repellent spray from a pet supply store and spray the little lady. DO NOT TRUST any preparation for the last ten days of the heat period.

- Chlorophyll pills given orally to a bitch in heat are recommended by some breeders. Check local pet supply stores for more information.

ROCK HOUNDS

- Dogs that are bored often collect, chew, or swallow rocks.

- If the owner has been handling rocks in a garden, the dog may feel it is an acceptable action and may try to help by carrying small rocks in his mouth. He may accidentally swallow one.

- Substitute chew bones.

- Spray oil of citronella, mixed with water, on all the rocks in the immediate vicinity.

- Swallowing rocks is a dangerous pastime and may require an operation. If all else fails, put a muzzle on until dog outgrows this habit.

RUNAWAYS

- If your dog is a vagabond, he is not a completely happy dog. He is searching for something — probably companionship.

- Adopt another animal to keep him company.

- Give your dog more attention. Take him in the car, go on walks, etc.

- A male dog may get the scent of a female in heat and nothing short of confinement will keep him from wandering off.

- Females in season often stray from home.

- SEE Chaining and Fencing, pages 86, 90.

SCRATCHERS

- If your dog scratches on the door, tack a piece of emery cloth over the area he scratches. This preserves the paint or wood and files the nails at the same time.

When I bark to get in
 You always get sore...
And equally irate
 When I scratch on the door.

- Try tying several tin cans together and fasten to the door. As he scratches the door, the noise will discourage him.

SELF-MUTILATION

- Dogs chew feet, tails, etc. for no apparent reason. If parasites can be ruled out, other factors may be considered, such as, boredom, loneliness, and stress. Try to find the answer.

- Begin a program of exercise, socialization, and obedience classes.

- Substitute chew bones for feet.

- When caught in the act, distract dog with noise such as dropping a metal object or using a shrill whistle. Follow with praise.

SKUNK ODOR

- Eliminate odor by rinsing with diluted cider vinegar.

- Bathe in tomato juice.

- Bathe the dog in Micrin mouthwash.

- First, put Murine or some ophthalmic product in the eyes. Sponge the dog with a Clorox solution (one gallon water, ¼ cup of Clorox) and leave on for five minutes. Rinse off and follow with a deodorant shampoo. For a very thick coat, saturation may be necessary.

- Make a solution of 4 ounces of ammonia to 2 quarts of water. Soak the dog and leave on for five minutes. Rinse well, shampoo, and rinse again.

URINE IN THE HOUSE

- Studies reveal objectionable urine markings in the house by male dogs is sometimes reduced or eliminated by castration.

- Punishment, strangers, eye contact, etc. may trigger submissive urination and the dog is unaware he is doing it. NEVER punish the dog. Set up positive situations.

- If a house-broken dog suddenly starts urinating in the house, clean the soiled area with an odor neutralizer. It eradicates the odor, thus eliminating the temptation. The next step is to take the dog outside more frequently. Be sure to praise profusely when he cooperates.

WAKE-UP

- Does your dog, eager for a new day of fun, wake you up before the alarm goes off? Try this. On the first day, get up and clip his nails before the usual routine. Repeat this procedure the second day. Now, unless your dog loves pedicures, on the third day he'll wait until YOU are ready to get up.

WASTEBASKET

- Some dogs love to take paper out of a basket and tear and scatter it over the floor. Place several set mouse traps in the bottom of the wastebasket. The slightest motion springs them, and the noise should frighten and discourage the dog.

- Put a few drops of citronella or pennyroyal on a piece of tissue and drop in the wastebasket.

PUPPIES

I'm brooding in the pet shop
  When in walks this great guy.
I'll thank my stars forever
  That it's me he decides to buy.

BEDDING

- **Disposable Diapers**

  - For a super absorbent and sanitary bedding, put disposable diapers in whelping box for new-born pups.

- **Indoor-Outdoor Carpeting**

  - Many people are using this type of carpet for the puppy as it is easy to clean. However, there is a great DANGER. Some, not all, indoor-outdoor carpeting has been treated with a chemical to aid in cleaning. If the carpet has been treated and the puppy urinates, the combination of the two elements can cause a severe chemical burn and even death.

  - If there is swelling, itching or any allergic reaction to the dye, remove carpet immediately.

- **Shredded Paper**

  - Shredding newspaper takes time. If you contact large businesses where they shred their confidential material in a machine, you may be able to pick up the shredded paper which they store in heavy plastic bags.

- **Three-Layer Mattress**

  - To make a waterproof, absorbent, and comfortable mattress, use a plastic sheet on the bottom, newspapers in the middle, and cloth on top. The cloth prevents the printer's ink from discoloring the puppy's coat.

CHEWERS

- **Bitter Apple**

  - May be purchased in pet supply stores. This product, if sprayed on attractive articles, is an unpleasant but safe deterrent.

  I'm a little tiny puppy
  My teeth are pearly white.
  All that's in my mind right now
  Is to find something to bite.

- **Cayenne Pepper**

  - Discourage rug chewers by sprinkling the corners with red hot cayenne pepper.

- **Oil of Citronella**

  - A few drops of this odorous oil is enough to disenchant any little chewer.

- **Tabasco Sauce**

  - If the puppy starts to chew something he shouldn't, rub the spot with Tabasco Sauce.

- **Vicks**

  - Dab a little Vicks on items puppy delights to chew. Vicks doesn't stain and the chewer will be dismayed at the smell.

CHILDREN AND DOGS

- Never leave puppies and toddlers unattended.

- Some adult dogs are not reliable around children.

  I'll love that child, I'm sure
  If I come out of this alive.
  Right now, my only thought
  Is somehow to survive.

- Pregnant and nursing bitches may not be too tolerant of children.

CLEANUP SUPPLIES

- Unwoven cotton and rayon towels are excellent to dry off young puppies. They are inexpensive.

- **Source of Toweling**

  - Local linen suppliers sell, by the pound, towels which have become unsuitable to rent to motels, barbershops, etc.

  - Old ragged towels may be purchased by the pound from local beauty parlors or barbershops.

CONDITIONING AND TRAINING

- **Cars**

  - SEE Riding in a Car, page 188.

- **Clippers**

  - Clipper noise is often frightening to a puppy. Turn the clippers on when you are playing with him. Next step is to hold the puppy with clippers turned on. Speak soothingly to him. After all fear is erased, your grooming sessions with clippers will be trouble free. A stressful situation is thus eliminated!

    Introduce the clippers first
    In fun or in play
    And I won't be so nervous
    On grooming day.

- **Jet Flights**

  - That standard household appliance, your vacuum cleaner, can condition dogs for their first jet flight. The whine of the vacuum is comparable to the sound of the jets on takeoff and landing. Gradually introduce your puppies to the new sound and talk to them normally.

- **Leash Training**

  - SEE Leash Training, page 187.

- **Possessiveness**

  - While puppy is still young, pick up his dish while he is eating — or take anything, bone, toy, etc. from his mouth. If any sign of antagonism is shown, punish; otherwise, praise him profusely.

- **Radios**

  - Condition the puppies to noise by keeping a transistor radio turned on by the whelping box or puppy pen.

- **Stair-Climbing**

  - Many people living in a single-story dwelling don't realize the importance of training a puppy to climb stairs. In an emergency, how would you like to carry your 150-pound dog upstairs? Also introduce him to open stairways such as fire escapes.

DANGERS

- **Electric Refrigerator**

  - A tiny puppy was killed when it wiggled back of a refrigerator and got caught in the fan. Block off area to prevent this from happening to your new puppy.

- **High Places**

  - Never leave puppies unattended on a table or high place. Serious injury can result from a fall.

- **String**

  - Keep string and yarn away from puppies as it may cause a fatal intestinal blockage if swallowed.

- **Toys**

    - Playthings should be chosen carefully. Toys that are brittle, such as plastics, can break and leave sharp edges. Broken pieces can be swallowed.

      I can't tell the difference
      'Til it is far too late.
      Toys that break leave edges
      That will likely seal my fate.

- **Vulnerability**

    - Inquisitive puppies are vulnerable to dangers in the environment. Puppy proof your home by putting away all objects that can be broken, chewed, or swallowed.

DISCIPLINE

- Puppies should be trained to respond to your tone of voice. If however, you need something more persuasive, grab the dog by the ruff and shake forcefully. This was his mother's method of disciplining and is very effective.

- Never hit your puppy. Hands should be associated with kindness. If discipline is necessary, a rolled up newspaper won't harm him — it's the noise that works. Too much discipline of this nature, however, could turn your dog into a cringing pet.

- Punish your dog while the crime is being committed.

- If your dog jumps up, snaps, or barks, fill a water pistol and squirt squarely between the eyes.

DISHES

- **Elevated Dishes**

    - The hardest part of learning to eat is for the puppy to get his chin down. The process can be speeded up if you elevate the feeding pan to chin level. This can be done by taping (using double-face tape) two aluminum cake pans together, bottom to bottom. This discourages puppies from wading in their food.

- **Metal Trays**

    - For feeding puppies who are being weaned, try metal ice cube trays (with the dividers out). Split the puppies into groups and give each group a tray.

        Look at my little darlings
        At mealtime all in a row.
        Let's relax for a little while.
        Sit back and watch them grow.

        They don't tip and spill as easily as metal pie plates, and pups can line up on the sides. The trays are easily cleaned and scalded without breakage.

FEEDING

- **Bottle Feeding Position**

    - If bottle feeding is necessary, the position of the puppy is important. Put the puppy on his back in your lap. Roll up a towel and place it where he can push against it with his feet. Do not hold the bottle too high and be sure the opening to the nipple is always covered with milk so that no air will be sucked in by the pup. After feeding, a puppy can be burped just like a baby—this may help prevent colic.

- **Forced Feeding**

    - If a dog is sick or off his feed and forced feeding is necessary, use an ordinary soft rubber ear syringe. The capacity is much greater than an eye dropper. The soft rubber will not hurt his gums. The tip can be cut off so that egg yolk, cereal, and even thinned hamburger can be fed quickly and in sufficient quantity to keep the dog in condition.

    - The best and safest method to administer food by syringe is to make a pocket in his cheek as you do for liquid medicines. Feed small amounts and massage the throat to induce swallowing.

- **Instant Puppy Meal**

    - Grind dry dog food in the blender to make a puppy meal. It can be ground to a fine powder for thickening a gruel.

- **Orphan Puppies**

  - Never feed newborn puppies ordinary or powdered milk.

  - Simulated canine milk is available at veterinary hospitals or pet supply stores.

  - Feed every three to four hours.

  The world is so big
  And I am so small...
  Without you beside me
  I won't make it at all.

  - A good homemade formula can be made by mixing equal parts of evaporated milk and water. Add an egg yolk and one tablespoon of Karo syrup or honey.

- **Picky Eaters**

  - Add salt and onion powder to the food.

  - Try spreading a thin film of butter or margarine around the rim of the feeding dish.

  - A little canned cat food will tempt most picky eaters. Just mix in enough with his regular meal for "odor appeal."

  - Do not separate the picky eater from the other puppies because you fear the strong ones will eat all the food. Many times all the puppy needs is competition. Watch carefully.

- **Warnings**

  - Do not permit strenuous exercise or play after eating.

  - Do not allow excessive drinking, especially after a meal.

FLOORING

- Outdoor carpet in the play pen gives the puppy better traction. Soiled carpet can be hung on the clothesline and washed with a hose. (WARNING: See Indoor-Outdoor Carpeting, page 153.)

- Disposable bedding provides excellent footing for your puppy.

- Local newspaper plants often have newsprint roll ends — plain, unprinted paper as it comes from the mill. Puppies don't get tattletale gray from the ink.

- Many poor hindquarters are created by slippery floors. Mix pumice in pool paint and apply to slippery linoleum in exercise area.

GROOMING

- **Bathing**

  - It is not recommended to bathe tiny puppies. However, an occasion may arise. It is not the water that harms them, but the harsh soaps on delicate skin and the possibility of getting chilled.

  - Use a mild shampoo and rinse well. Dry thoroughly and keep the puppy in a warm room out of drafts for several hours.

  - Puppies may be dry-cleaned in winter weather. Cornmeal or commercial dry shampoo may be used.

- **Brushing**

  - An excellent grooming tool for young puppies is a bristle vegetable brush. It is small, curved, and all parts of the puppy are easily brushed.

- **Ears**

  - Puppy ears should be cleaned regularly but not with water. Apply mineral or baby oil with cotton. As puppy's ears are even more sensitive than your own, proceed very carefully.

HANDLING

- The best way to hold or carry your pet is to place one hand under the animal's chest and the other under his back end for support.

- Putting the puppy down on the floor should be done as carefully as when you picked him up. Serious injury to legs, shoulders, or head can arise if puppy hits the floor with a thud.

- Never lift a puppy by the skin of the neck. Put your hands under his body and support him.

HOUSEBREAKING

- **Age**

  - Housebreaking should begin around six weeks of age.

    You humans could be
    Much more consistent
    Cause to get my way
    I can be persistent.

  - The older the puppy is the easier it is to train as the muscles for elimination are more developed.

  - By twelve weeks of age, the puppy should be fully trained — give or take a few puddles.

- **Crate Training**

  - The crate is probably the best training tool available for housebreaking. Animals in the wild keep their dens clean so it is natural for the puppy to refrain from messing the crate "den" if at all possible. Take the puppy outside at regular intervals, and he will learn to wait. Before long he will be reliable, but YOU must keep to a schedule.

- Familiar Spot

  - Decide on the best spot in your yard for the puppy to eliminate. Take the puppy there each time.

- **Frequency**

3	months of age	—	at least six trips outside daily.
6	months of age	—	at least four times a day.
12 +	months of age	—	three times a day.

- **Length of Time**

  - It takes four to six weeks to housebreak an average dog.

  - The length of time depends on the dog's age, breed, intelligence, and the owner's sense of responsibility.

- **Minimize Accidents**

  - Do not let the puppy wander from room to room. Keep him confined to his bed or a corner where you can watch him.

    This world is so big
    And I am so little...
    Won't somebody show me
    The right place to piddle?

  - Take the puppy outside the minute he wakes up.

  - The habit of regular elimination does much to prevent medical problems later.

  - Take the puppy outside as soon as he eats.

  - Each time your puppy has an accident, scold severely and immediately take him outside. Praise profusely if he relieves himself, then return to the house immediately.

- **Paper Training**

  - Paper the floor of his area wall to wall. Pick up soiled paper and put down fresh. Decide on one area and place urine-stained paper there. Gradually reduce area covered by newspaper.

  - Should a puppy relieve himself in front of you and not on the paper say "No," and pick him up, and place on the paper, and immediately praise.

- **Praise**

  - There is no reason whatsoever for a dog to go outside except to please his owner. Therefore, tell the puppy or even older dogs how wonderful they are. They really want to please you.

- **Signal Word**

  - Decide on a word or a phrase to use when you want your puppy to eliminate. Use such words or phrases as "Do it," "Do your business," etc. each time you take the dog out so he will associate the act with the word. It will be less time-consuming later. This method is helpful on trips or when you have a schedule to maintain.

- **Worms**

  - Worms can contribute to a dog's inability to be house-broken.

INTRODUCTION TO NEW HOME

- Allow puppy time to relieve himself before entering the house.

- Do not take a new puppy out of the yard until he has had his permanent shots.

- At night, place a clock with a loud tick near the bed.

- A radio, playing softly near his bed, gives your puppy the feeling that he's not entirely alone.

- A puppy will miss his mother and litter mates. A jar, with a rubber ring in the lid, filled with warm water, and covered with a towel, is comforting.

- On the first day in his new home, weigh the puppy so you will have a guide as to whether you are under- or over-feeding him.

- It's a temptation but don't let members of the family over-whelm the new puppy. Be gentle and quiet and let him get ac-quainted first with the new environment, then gradually intro-duce him to his new family.

- In a cold climate, spring and summer is the ideal time to ac-quire a puppy. Housebreaking is much easier. Christmas pup-pies are not always an ideal gift. The excitement and pressures of the holidays do not allow for proper environment and train-ing.

NAMES

- One or two syllable names are preferable as the sound will carry.

- **Avoid**

  - Names that ridicule or date your dog.

  - Names that end in "o" as names with the long "o" may be confused with "No."

  - Names that start with "S." The dog may confuse his name with the commands of "sit," "stand," "stay."

  - Names that indicate a bad temperament such as "Killer," "Nipper," or "Snapper." If your dog does bite someone, it would be difficult to defend him with such a moniker.

- **Elements of a Good Dog Name**

  - Can be shouted sharply as part of a command.

  - Should be an apt name.

  - Can be crooned for sweet talking the dog.

    When you give us our monikers
    Take a tip from me and be wise.
    We're stuck with it for life,
    So consider our future size.

  - Should be distinctive enough to set the dog apart from other dogs and thus avoid confusion.

- **Sources**

  - American Stud Book
  - Dictionary
  - Dog magazines
  - Foreign dictionary of your breed's origin
  - Racing forms
  - Show catalogs

- **Suggestions**

  - Alliterations
  - Breed characteristics
  - Designate a locale
  - Flowers
  - Jewels
  - Mythology
  - Names from literature
  - Notable figures from history
  - Nursery rhymes
  - Origin of breed
  - Take-off on names of owners

- SEE APPENDIX, Names

PUPPY PENS

- **Baby Playpen**

  - A discarded playpen is an easy and safe method for confining puppies. Be sure, however, to fasten plastic wiring outside of the slats so puppy can't get caught or wiggle out.

- **Barricades**

  - An adjustable window screen across the door is an adequate barricade for small dogs yet allows people to step over with ease.

- A baby gate is excellent for keeping a puppy confined.

- **Outside Exercise Pens**

  - For very small puppies, a roll of short, decorative fencing is light and easy to move. The short plastic stakes can be pushed in by hand. It is high enough to keep little puppies in, yet low enough to let the mother (medium or large dog) visit her family.

  - Commercial exercise pens are available at pet supply stores.

- **Pegboard Play Pen**

  - Take four pieces of pegboard — size depends on size of puppies — and lace together with nylon rope. Easy to store for future use.

- **Wading Pool**

  - A hard plastic wading pool makes a perfect pen for very small puppies. Line with paper. Easily cleaned.

- **Wire Bottom Pens**

  - Puppies raised in wire-bottom pens may not make a distinction between their pen and floor registers when playing in the house!

PURCHASING A PUPPY

- Don't buy trouble or heartache. Check the puppy carefully on the following points:

  - **Abdomen.** A distended abdomen may indicate worms, improper diet, or malformation.

  - **Coat.** Patches with no hair may indicate mange, ringworm, or eczema.

  - **Deafness.** Stand behind the dog and make noises. If after several attempts, he ignores the sounds, he is probably deaf.

- **Distemper.** Indicated by running eyes and nose, diarrhea, and a temperature.

- **Ears.** Should be pink and smooth with no sign of infection.

- **Hernia.** It may disappear or may require an operation. Check with veterinarian for his opinion.

- **Listless.** May indicate possible problems or may be as simple as a need for another worming.

- **Rash.** Check inside of legs and abdomen.

- **Rickets.** Indicated by crooked legs and enlarged bones.

- **Shy or Fearful.** Could indicate a temperament problem or the result of a recent traumatic experience.

REST

- Puppies, like babies, need a lot of rest and sleep; otherwise, they may become ill. Do not disturb a sleeping puppy.

STAINS AND CLEANUP

- Absorb excess moisture. Pour club soda over the spot and allow it to remain for one minute. Blot up the moisture with rags or paper towels. Do not use newspapers as the ink may stain the carpet.

- Blot up urine. Make up a solution of ¼ cup of white vinegar in a pint of water and saturate the spot. Let stand for five minutes. Blot up the moisture and repeat.

I wiggle and I squirm
  And may wet upon the floor.
Teach me patiently and gently
  And I'll soon go to the door.

- It is important to get rid of past urinary and excretory odors on floors and carpets so the dog will not be tempted to relieve himself on the same spot. An odor neutralizer is available in pet supply stores and pharmacies. Ordinary cleaning products DO NOT neutralize the odors. Follow directions on bottle.

TEETHING

- Give chew bones or ice cubes for teething discomfort.

- Put a wet twisted wash cloth in the freezer. When it is stiff, give to the puppy to chew on — the coldness will numb the gums.

- For the young puppy who is teething and chewing on everything, rub and massage his swollen gums with oil of cloves.

- Don't leave puppies alone when they are teething — they can be small demolition crews.

- Milk teeth shed between three to five months. If temporary teeth do not come out by themselves, consult your veterinarian.

TEMPERATURE

- The average normal temperature of a puppy is 102.5 degrees. A temperature of 103 degrees is no cause for alarm but anything above this may indicate a serious problem.

TOYS

- **Baby's Clutch Ball**

  - A baby's clutch ball allows little mouths to hold and carry large balls. The surface is not smooth and they can get their teeth around the ridges.

    That durable squeaky toy
    Gives me hours of action
    So what if my family
    Is driven to distraction.

- **Blue Jeans**

  - Cut strips from old blue jeans. Tie several knots.

- **Neckties**

  - Old neckties are a safe toy for puppies to enjoy.

- **Panty Hose**

  - Panty hose tied in knots is a good toy for a puppy.

- **Paper Throwaways**

  - Puppies enjoy playing with paper throwaways, such as: empty paper towel roll, empty tissue roll, milk carton, old box, empty salt box after metal spout has been removed.

- **Plastic Bottles**

  - Thoroughly clean a plastic bottle. Tie a sock to handle so that your puppy can pull it around the house. If he starts to chew the plastic into bits, replace with a new bottle.

- **Socks**

  - An old sock filled with rags and knotted at the top will provide many hours of happy chewing.

- **Squeaky Toys**

  - Such toys can be hazardous if whistle is swallowed.

- **Toy Box**

  - To avoid clutter, provide a toy box for your puppy. He'll love searching for that one particular treasure.

VACCINATIONS

- Puppies are born without immunity protection to infectious diseases; however, the mother's first milk, called colostrum, contains antibodies against infection. This protecton lasts from a couple of weeks to possibly eight weeks. During this time, the puppy should not be exposed to other dogs or taken out in public. At the end of this period, take your puppy to the veterinarian for immunizations.

- Your veterinarian can give a single injection called D-H-L which is for distemper, infectious hepatitis and leptospirosis.

- **Distemper**

  - This serious dog disease is highly contagious. It is caused by an airborne virus or by direct contact.

- **Hepatitis**

  - Infectious Canine Hepatitis (ICH) is caused by a virus found in urine, feces, and saliva of infected animals. It is a contagious disease of the liver. This disease works so fast that a puppy may die before the seriousness of the illness is recognized.

- **Infectious Bronchitis** (Kennel Cough)

  - A self-limiting disease involving the trachea and bronchi. It is highly contagious and afflicted dogs should be isolated.

- **Leptospirosis**

  - A spirochetal disease that primarily affects the kidneys. It is infectious to humans (Weil's disease). It is spread by contact with the urine of the infected dog, by swimming, or drinking water contaminated with the infectious urine.

- **Parvovirus**

  - Canine parvovirus (CPV) is a new disease not recognized before 1978. It is now world-wide. Transmitted by a virus found in the feces of diseased animals. All dogs should be immunized for CPV — especially puppies.

- **Rabies**

  - Caused by the saliva of a rabid animal. This fatal disease affects the nervous system. The puppy should be vaccinated at 4-6 months and at three-year intervals.

- **Tetanus**

  - The tetanus bacteria is common around horse stables. This vaccination is advised if a dog is around these animals.

SKIN

Do you 'spose I itch
  Because my skin is dry?
Let's find a recommended remedy
  And give it a try.

ABSCESS

- Two types of abscess:

  1. Superficial. Indicated by white or yellow pus around the scab.

  2. Deep. Indicated by a soft, hot, and swollen area. The dog may have fever and loss of appetite.

- Abscesses may occur five to six days after an injury.

- Clip the hair around the swelling close to the skin.

- The wound should heal from the INSIDE toward the OUT-SIDE.

- Keep the wound open and clean until there is no sign of infection. Do not let scab form until the infection has cleared up.

- Thorough cleaning is necessary. Use a medicinal solution of hydrogen peroxide (3%) three times a day, or wash with soap and water and rinse well with clear water.

- Bathe in warm water to which Epsom Salts has been added (one tablespoon to a pint of water).

- If an abscess does not come to a head, apply hot towels to the area.

- The abscess should come to a head, burst, and heal. If this does not happen and a new abscess develops, consult a veterinarian.

ACNE

- Pimples appear on the chin under the collar and stomach.

- Acne may be caused by overactive sebaceous glands which have become infected.

- Clean out the pimple by squeezing and apply alcohol. If the condition continues, the veterinarian may prescribe antibiotics.

ALLERGY

- Allergy is caused by excessive sensitivity to certain substances such as dust, drugs, dyes, food, insecticides, insects, mold, nylon, weeds, and wool. These substances may be inhaled, ingested, or injected.

- The most serious allergic reaction would be anaphylactic shock frequently caused by injection of drugs or insect stings. Death may occur as a result of respiratory and circulatory failure.

- Less severe allergic reactions are manifested by hives, swelling, and intense itching which could lead to skin infections.

- Try to find the source of the allergen by the process of elimination. If this is not successful, treatment by a veterinarian is necessary. SEE Dermatitis, pages 173-175.

BRUISES

- Small blood vessels which have ruptured result in a reddish-bluish discoloration of the injured area.

- Severe bruises may result in large hematomas which will require professional attention.

- Bruises are sensitive and often accompanied by swelling.

- If the bruise is recent (within 12 hours), apply cold packs.

- The bruise will usually disappear in a few days.

CALLUSES

- A hardened or thickened part of the skin where elbows, hocks, head, and sometimes tail come in contact with a hard surface. Treatment is only needed if calluses become infected.

- To prevent calluses, provide your dog with a mattress made of foam padding, carpet, or folded blanket.

- Oil, lanolin, or vaseline relieves dryness and stimulates hair growth.

DANDRUFF

- It is small, white, slightly greasy flakes often associated with a "dry" form of seborrhea without any inflammation.

- Dandruff may be caused by too many baths or insufficient rinsing. The remaining soap dries and irritates the skin.

- If the problem is caused by lack of fat in the diet, add one teaspoon of bacon fat or vegetable oil to one cup of dry dog food.

- Recommended vitamin therapy for dandruff is A, D, and B-6.

- Vigorous brushing daily will help.

DERMATITIS

- Three comon types of dermatitis

  1. Allergic inhalent

  2. Contact

  3. Flea bites

- **Allergic Inhalent Dermatitis**

  - Severe itching in a generalized area.

  - Supersensitiveness to dust, feathers, mold, pollen, or wool.

  - It may be inherited.

  - Eliminate all possible allergens from the environment.

  - Bathe the dog to remove any allergens on the coat and skin.

  - Apply Calamine lotion or hydrogen peroxide to irritations.

  - If home treatment is unsuccessful see your veterinarian.

- **Contact Dermatitis**

  - Contracted by coming in contact with an irritating substance such as dyes, flea collars, grasses, insecticides, soaps, poison ivy, or wool.

  - Symptoms are severe scratching and inflamed areas.

  - By the process of elimination, remove any suspected substance.

  - Apply a soothing lotion to the affected areas. If the problem does not clear up, see your veterinarian.

- **Flea Bite Dermatitis**

  - A parasitic skin disease that is easy to diagnose but difficult to cure.

  - Characterized by severe itching, especially at base of tail, around the neck and inside of legs. Crusty areas that may become infected result in hair loss.

  - The first requisite is to eliminate fleas in the dog's environment by spraying the lawn, dog runs, patio, and doghouse with a recommended insecticide. FOLLOW DIRECTIONS.

- If your pet is a house dog, do some or all of the following: Vacuum the rugs thoroughly and burn the contents of the bag. Wash all bedding. Use a flea bomb, fogger, or an insecticidal powder.

- Bathe your dog to remove infestation of fleas.

- Ask your veterinarian to recommend an insecticidal dip, powder, collar, medallion, or spray.

- Some breeders recommend brewer's yeast and garlic.

ECZEMA

- Dermatitis is a skin inflammation having a known cause, while eczema is a similar condition with an unknown origin.

- Eczema is of two varieties, dry and moist.

- Dry eczema is characterized by intense itching, dryness of the skin and coat with hair loss.

- In moist eczema, sometimes called "hot spots" or "weeping mange" there is intense itching, pustular lesions, edema, redness, and thickening of the skin. These spots generally start at the hips in front of the tail and increase in size.

- **Tips from Breeders:**

  - Soak the spot daily with a solution of two teaspoons of household bleach added to a quart of water. If there is no improvement, use a stronger solution.

    I see myriads of skin creams
    When we're watching TV.
    Do you suppose one of them
    Would work for me?

  - Genetian violet is a fungicide and antiseptic agent that has been successfully used for hot spots. It stains but, eventually, wears away.

  - Goodwinol Ointment for mange also helps to control the itching. The first application usually aids in the formation of a scab within 12 hours.

- The pesticidal shampoo, using kerosene is very helpful. SEE Pesticidal Shampoo, page 71.

- Powdered varieties of athlete's foot preparations help relieve and sometimes cure this skin condition.

- Eczema responds well to topical ointments containing anti-inflammatory drugs.

- Sponge the area twice daily with hydrogen peroxide (3%).

- Dogs often become frantic with itching. Ask the veterinarian about a mild tranquilizer.

- If the itching is intense the dog will scratch and set up an infection. Put an Elizabethan collar on him. SEE Bandage or Wound Protection, page 47.

HAIR LOSS (Alopecia)

- Baldness may result from several inflammatory disorders or without any apparent skin disease.

- Alopecia may be congenital or acquired.

- Loss of hair is a frequent sign of a specific skin disease such as mange and ringworm or disorder of the thyroid or pituitary.

- In treatment, diet and cleanliness are important. Thyroid therapy may be indicated.

- If topical medication is used, it should be nonirritating and rapid drying such as one that contains salicylic acid.

HEMATOMA

- A tumor or swelling that contains blood.

- If there is an injury to the ear flap due to a bite or wound, blood may collect in the area. It is often necessary for a veterinarian to drain off the blood from the swelling in order to prevent scarring.

HIVES

- Hives are indicated by eruptions of small bumps all over the body or swelling of the lips and area around the eyes and ears. The problem often develops and disappears rapidly.

- The cause is an allergic reaction to certain plants, foodstuffs, vaccines, and serums.

- By the process of elimination, try to determine the allergenic cause and remove it from the dog's environment.

- Antihistamines may be prescribed by your veterinarian.

- Cold packs of water, vinegar, or alcohol may be applied.

- Usually the hives disappear without treatment.

MANGE

- **Demodectic (Red Mange)**

  - A disease caused by worm-like mites. It is most common in young dogs. The problem is more easily seen in short-haired ones. Examination of long-haired dogs is vital as this is a serious skin disease.

  - Positive diagnosis can only be made by examining skin scrapings or material from pustules under the microscope.

  - Bald spots generally occur around the eyes, elbows, hocks, and tail.

  - As the disease progresses, the skin becomes red with blood and serum oozes from the affected areas.

  - Demodectic mange is a persistent disease and often responds poorly to treatment. Don't wait too long before seeking professional help. It can be fatal.

  - Flea powder containing rotenone or extract of derrin root in oil helps keep new areas from being affected.

- **Sarcoptic Mange (Scabies)**

  - It is highly contagious. Humans may become infected. Keep dog isolated.

  - Microscopic examination of skin scrapings is necessary to make positive identification.

  - The symptoms include intense itching and loss of hair.

  - Apply insecticides recommended by your veterinarian.

  - Give medicated baths.

  - Rub on sulphur ointments.

  - Use dips containing lindane.

PSORIASIS

- A chronic skin disease characterized by silvery-white scales. It is often called "elephant skin" as the skin becomes thick, coarse, and gray.

- Psoriasis does not affect the general health. The cause of the disease is unknown, but diet may be a contributing factor.

- There is no drug that will cure psoriasis but your veterinarian will recommend topical applications to ease the condition.

- Frequent baths to which baking soda has been added to the water is helpful. Dry thoroughly and apply a calamine lotion.

- Some cases have responded well to ultra-violet light or sun exposure. Psoriasis usually abates during the summer months.

- Vitamin D has proved beneficial, especially in the winter.

RINGWORM

- A fungus disease characterized by circular patches of gray or brownish-yellow crusts. The disease starts small but gradually increases in size. It can only be identified under a microscope. This disease can be transmitted to humans.

- Grooming equipment used on a dog with ringworm should be sterilized before using on other dogs.

- Griseofulvin tablets should clear up the fungal invasion in three or four weeks.

- Use antifungal dips or iodine shampoo on the seventh and fourteenth day of the griseofulvin treatment.

- For small areas, use a cream called Tinactin (containing tolnaftate) for three weeks.

- Medicines containing iodine or salicylic acid are helpful in controlling ringworm.

In some ways,
An itch is worse than pain
It must be my skin
For a bug you've looked in vain.

- Reinfection will occur unless cleanliness is maintained.

- Paint spot with tincture of iodine.

- Scrub areas where dog frequents and burn old bedding.

SOLAR DERMATITIS

- An inflammation of the skin of the nose which causes peeling and depigmentation.

- Keep the dog out of the sunlight.

- Darken the skin above the nose by tatooing.

- Cortisone ointments relieve the itching and inflammation.

- Apply sun-screening preparations.

TUMORS

- A tumor is an abnormal growth of tissue. There are two types: Benign tumors which grow slowly and are confined to one part of the body. Malignant tumors, commonly called cancer, which grow rapidly and spread to other parts of the body.

- Unfortunately internal tumors may grow quite large before an owner is aware of it. Those on the body and in the mouth may be detected early if periodic examinations are made.

- Skin tumors are the most common form of cancer in a dog. Fortunately, the majority are benign.

- Female dogs are more prone to mammary cancer than any other type; especially those that are unspayed — or spayed after their first season. A large tumor will appear on the breast. If such a lump appears, see your veterinarian immediately.

- Old male dogs commonly have tumors around the anus. Partial control of these tumors can be done with female hormone injections but the only satisfactory answer is surgery. These tumors are generally cancerous and spread very rapidly.

- Treatment for cancer may be cobalt treatment, chemotherapy, radiation therapy, and surgery.

- No growth should be disregarded, especially those that grow rapidly. Your dog's life may be saved by prompt surgical removal or treatment.

WARTS

- Warts are growths that appear on the skin or inside the mouth.

- Puppies are more prone to the soft warts on the inside of the mouth. If they interfere with eating or cause excessive flow of saliva, they should be removed.

- Hard warts on the skin of the body generally occur in older dogs. Removal is not necessary unless the wart causes a problem.

TRAINING

You'll find that teaching me
Isn't such a feat
If you make the periods...
Frequent, short, and sweet.

ACHIEVEMENT

- Many problems arise because dogs need more from life than love and pampering. Dogs are happiest when they can perform small tasks such as carrying in the paper or bringing slippers to you. Obeying commands to "Come," "Sit," "Down," "Stay," is another way to give dogs a feeling of achievement.

BARKING DOGS

- Have an assistant help you with this training. Door bells and telephones often excite a dog and he starts barking. Put a training collar and lead on the dog. When a bell rings, allow one bark, then grab the lead, give a sharp jerk, and say, "No Bark." Repeat until he understands.

- This suggestion came from a breeder of dogs inclined to bark a great deal. She took masking tape and wrapped it many times around the muzzle of the dog, leaving the mouth slightly open. She kept using the word, "Tape" as she wound. It took her fastest dog 10 minutes to get the tape off and she promptly re-wrapped the muzzle. After a few sessions of this, all she had to say was "Tape" and the dog was quiet.

- Use a correctly fitted leather muzzle every time the dog barks unnecessarily with the admonition "No Bark." This annoying habit is soon discouraged.

- Muzzle the dog with an old nylon stocking wrapped around the dog's mouth and securely knotted at the back of the neck. The muzzle should be loose enough so the dog can breathe and drink easily.

- Use a large water gun and squirt in the dog's face as you say "No Bark." Timing is important.

- If close enough, throw a container of water in his face. At the same time, say, "No Bark."

- If your housedog barks without provocation, put him in a room alone or make him lie down in his own corner. He will soon associate his annoying barking with your displeasure.

- Do not overtrain so that your dog will never bark. He is good burglar insurance. His barking could alert you to a house fire or other emergencies.

BITERS

- Obedience training is more effective if instructor is trained to work with problem dogs.

- If your dog is a biter, put a muzzle on him and take him around people. If he lashes out, jerk and scold him severely and try again. By muzzling the dog, you and others will be less fearful and can concentrate on the training. Eventually, remove the muzzle and practice around people and dogs that are aware of the problem.

BOUNDARIES

- Dogs can be taught to stay within an unfenced area. However, unless the training is consistent, thorough, and demanding, there is no guarantee your dog will not cross that invisible boundary to follow a bitch in heat, a pack of dogs, or some other enticement. It's up to you to train him properly.

  Boundaries by myself
  I cannot discern.
  Show me many times
  And maybe I'll learn.

  1. Put a training collar and leash on the dog and walk the boundaries. The instant one paw steps over the "line" give a severe jerk and say "No." Do this for a week.

2. For the second week, use a long line to allow greater freedom. One infraction earns a severe jerk and "NO."

3. In the third week, set up distractions on the other side of the boundary line, such as, cats, dogs, children, food.

4. If all goes well, remove leash but continue with distractions.

5. For the "pièce de résistance," hide from the dog and have a friend walk by with a bitch in heat (for males) or several active dogs that are playing and romping. Award and praise profusely if he resists temptation.

This training MUST BE consistent and emphatic with frequent refresher courses.

BREED DIFFERENCES

- In training, do not expect the same results from all dogs. The different breeds were bred for various purposes. Some dogs work well with man, others work more independently. Dogs run the gamut from extreme sensitivity to hard-headedness and obstinacy. If you are planning to train your dog, get a book on your particular breed to better understand his individual characteristics. Training is fascinating because of the unique singularities of each breed.

When training us pets
  You should keep in mind
That because of heredity
  We're not all of one kind.

CAT KILLERS

- Use a prong collar and a long line about 25 feet long. Stand 30 feet from the cat. Allow the dog to lunge at the cat. When he gets to the end of the rope yell "NO." The collar will pinch and he will probably get a bad spill. Call him to you and pet and praise. Repeat many times. It will take patience, but he should get the message.

- If everything else fails, go to a trainer who KNOWS how to use a shock collar. The dog and cat will be put together. When the dog approaches the cat he will be shocked by remote control.

CHASING CARS

- Put a training collar and lead on the dog. Stand by a busy street. The instant he lunges at a car, give a severe jerk on the lead and say, "No." This will take patience but will pay off.

Strange things that move
Are always fair game,
But my master says
They could kill or maim.

- Have a friend drive you slowly down the street. When the dog starts chasing the car, dump a bucket of water on him.

- When the dog starts chasing the car, throw out of the window a number of tin cans that have been tied together.

- SEE Chasing Cars, page 141.

"COME"

- If your dog doesn't come when called, there is a good reason. He may be associating the command with something unpleasant such as punishment, confinement, trip to the veterinarian, medication, etc. To overcome this problem, make the association with the command a pleasant one.

- Fasten a long line (15-25 feet) to the collar. Let the dog wander around for a while, then call him. If he ignores you, jerk the line and haul him in with the command "Come." Praise him and give a little treat. Repeat. If he is responding well, take off the line and say "Come" followed by praise. However, if he disobeys, replace the line and practice some more.

- Keep your voice happy and enthusiastic and your dog will respond in a happy and enthusiastic manner.

- Never call a dog to you for punishment or a scolding. If he misbehaves, go to him. Should he run off do not chase him but go in the opposite direction and he will follow.

- Tidbits may be used as an enticement but do not rely on them alone.

CRATES

- Unfortunately, many people associate a crate with a cage for wild animals and think it is cruel. NOTHING COULD BE FURTHER FROM THE TRUTH. Just

  In time of stress
  *   It's my safe retreat*
  To relax and know
  *   I'm not under your feet.*

  as your own room is where you go for rest and security, so the dog's crate is his very own unassailable refuge. If properly trained, he will prefer it. Even with the door open, he will feel more secure.

- Don't push the dog in and shut the door. Let the dog see you put a toy or a goodie inside, or even his dish. Leave the door open. Once the dog gets his treasure or eats from the dish, let him come out. Do this several times. Praise him profusely. Next, when he goes inside, quietly shut the door and speak encouragingly to him. Leave the door shut for a very short time. As you continue this training, keep the door shut for longer periods of time. Give him a chew bone, shut the door and go to another part of the house and stay for about ten minutes. By this time, he will be happy and contented. To him the crate has many happy associations — food, praise, and toys.

- SEE Crates, pages 86, 161, 198.

CURB STOPS

- If you stop to wait for the light to change as you walk your dog, practice making him sit. This habit may save your dog's life should the leash or fastener break or he slips his collar.

CURB YOUR DOG

- A term and practice used by responsible dog owners. When walking your dog on city streets, train him to use the curb to eliminate.

DON'T TOUCH

- Train your dog to "freeze" when you say, "Don't Touch." This command could prevent a dog from eating poisonous food and plants, attacking a smaller animal, or swallowing a harmful or valuable object.

- Put a lead on the dog sitting in front of you. Give him a bite of his favorite food. Toss another piece on the floor and as he goes for it, give a strong jerk on the leash and say, "Don't Touch." Practice until he knows the meaning of this command.

- Train your dog never to accept food from strangers.

- Do not allow your dog to pick up food off the street.

HEELING

- This term simply means your dog is walking by your side. The dog is trained to walk on your left side. This practice started when men used dogs to hunt. They carried the gun in the right hand and placed the dog on the left.

Basic commands
Are heel and stay.
To keep me safe
There's no other way.

  - Put a training collar and leash on your dog and have him sit on your left side. As you step out with your left foot, give the dog's name and say "Heel." If he doesn't move instantly, give a short jerk to the leash.

  - Don't let your dog take YOU for a walk. You must be in control. If he forges ahead, give sharp, short jerks backward and say, "NO." If your dog is very rambunctious, do not continue to walk in a straight line but make several changes of direction, using sharp jerks as you turn. You could also try circling right and left and do about turns to keep him more alert. When you stop, your dog should sit.

  - Some dogs will lag. Give short jerks forward and speak encouragingly to him. Be over-enthusiastic for this type of dog. Talk as you walk, encourage, and praise.

JUMPING ON PEOPLE

- When your dog jumps up, grab the front feet and hold on. Talk nicely but hang on until his greatest desire is to get all four feet on the ground. Repeat each time he jumps up. He'll soon get the message.

- "Knee-in-the-Chest" method doesn't always solve the problem of jumping as it can stimulate excitable dogs. It is also possible to hurt a dog if too much force is used. When you raise your knee and your dog hits it, a barrier is created and he is not able to support himself. This may discourage him after a time.

- "Annie Oakley" Method. Keep a "loaded" water pistol in your pocket. When the dog jumps up, squirt a stream of water in his face and say "No Jump."

LEASH TRAINING

- Some puppies rebel at the wearing of a collar and leash. Begin with a light weight collar and let him get used to that. Next fasten a light weight cord to the collar and let him trail it around the house. After a time, pick up the cord and call him to you, rewarding him with praise and a treat. Before long he will accept the leash and collar.

- If puppy dislikes to walk on the leash, pick him up, snap on the lead and carry away from the house or familiar surroundings. Put the puppy down and walk back to the house making enticing sounds. He will probably follow you and forget about the leash.

- Training the puppy to accept a collar and leash calls for patience and understanding. Being too forceful will only frighten him and build up fears that will make future training more difficult.

OBEDIENCE TRAINING

- It is possible to obedience train your own dog. Obtain a good training book, make lesson plans, and set up a regular schedule for practice. However, participating in a class may give better results. You will receive suggestions for correction, encouragement, and the incentive to practice. Your dog will benefit from the association and socialization with other dogs.

- To locate an obedience training club in your area, write to the American Kennel Club. SEE Appendix.

- Ask your veterinarian, pet supply store, or breeder to recommend a trainer.

- Before enrolling your dog in a training class, attend a session and observe the techniques being used.

PUNISHMENT

- A dog severely punished will not hate but will fear you. Fear can cause serious problems physically and psychologically.

- Severe punishment is indicated only on two occasions:

  1. If your dog precipitates a dog fight.

  2. If he attacks, without cause, a person.

RIDING IN A CAR

- Introduce your dog to a car gradually. Put the dog in a crate and let him adjust to his surroundings. Turn on the engine but do not drive. Talk quietly. If dog is nervous, repeat for several days. Next take a short drive. Gradually, introduce sounds of window washers, radio, fans, etc. Now take a trip to the service station. Correct the dog if he acts too protective of his kennel-on-wheels.

- If the dog is riding in the car with you but not in a crate, insist at the very beginning where his place is in the car. Do not allow jumping back and forth, barking at people, dogs, or sounds.

STAIR TRAINING

- To prevent dangerous falls on the stairs, train your dog to stay on one side of you as you go up and down the steps. Put the dog on a lead and practice until he knows what is expected of him.

STAYS

- It is better and quicker to teach your dog these exercises if you put him on a leash. You will have greater control.

- Sit-Stay

  1. When the dog is sitting beside you, place your hand in front of his face, and command, "Stay."

  2. Pivot first in front of the dog, then back to his side. Do this a number of times.

  3. If the dog attempts to stand, pull UP on the leash and press DOWN on the hindquarters. Use the command, "Sit."

  4. When you feel the dog understands this command, back away, a few steps at a time. Go to the end of the leash. When he appears steady, walk the distance of the leash around the dog.

  5. When you are positive the dog will not move, drop the leash and walk about 30 feet away. Be sure to command, "Stay."

  6. If he moves, say "No!" and put him in the exact spot he was in previously.

  7. Eventually you will be able to go out of sight, and he will remain in the sitting position.

- **Down-Stay**

    1. Have the dog lie down by your left side. Place the palm of your hand in front of his face and command, "Stay."

        In training me
        You'll save us grief,
        If you make the sessions
        Frequent, regular and brief.

    2. Pivot in front of the dog, then back to his side. Do this a number of times.

    3. If the dog attempts to get up, grab the collar or leash near the fastener and with quick, sharp jerks toward the floor get him again in the down position. Repeat "Stay" so he will make the correct association.

    4. When the dog appears steady, back away a few steps at a time to the end of the leash. Holding the leash, circle the dog.

    5. If you are confident the dog will stay at 6 feet, drop the leash and walk away—about 30 feet. Give the "Stay" command. If he moves, promptly return him to the original spot.

    6. Practice the Down-Stay until he remains in this position for about five minutes. When he is really steady, go out of sight to test his staying capability.

TABLE TRAINING

- This training is invaluable for trips to the veterinarian and should be started at a very early age.

- A grooming table is ideal but any large table will do. If it is a smooth table, place a rubber mat or blanket on surface so the dog does not slip and will feel more secure. Stand your dog on this table several times a day.

- Invite your friends and neighbors to place their hands on your dog while he is on the table. This trains your pet to tolerate being handled by strangers and veterinarians.

TRAINING COLLAR

- To get the full effect of a training collar (choke chain) it must be put on correctly. Take the chain and make a circle by dropping the chain through one of the rings. Put the free RING on the "Ring" finger of your left hand. Stand in front of your dog and slip the chain over the head. This method allows the chain to release without harming the dog.

TRAINING SESSIONS

- Work a puppy several times a day but not for more than five minute sessions.

- Older dogs may be worked three times a day. Each session can last from ten to fifteen minutes.

I like to learn
  But don't work me long,
Or I'll get bored
  And do it all wrong.

TRAINING TIPS

- Dogs react to their owner's moods. Never train unless YOU enjoy it.

- Commands should be short — preferably one word.

- Repetition is necessary but not to the point of boredom.

- The dog should never be allowed to disregard a single command. Once he gets away with disobedience he will attempt it again.

- Praise your dog for a good performance. He wants to please you and when he does, praise is his reward.

- Your voice must be enthusiastic and have a ring of authority.

- Build the dog's confidence by ending the training session on an exercise he does well.

- End each training session with a romp and a treat.

UNATTENDED DOGS

- Untrained dogs left alone can be a problem to neighbors by howling or barking. They can also be a problem to you by destructive behavior. Begin training early before your pet must be left alone.

- Leave the dog alone in a crate or room for ten minutes — gradually increasing the time. If he should bark or howl, bang on the door and say "No" but do not enter the room. At the end of the specified time, return to the dog and tell him what a good dog he is. Practice this until you can be sure he will accept your absence.

- It is best to start with puppies but an older dog will soon adjust, for he knows you will return.

VOCABULARY

- As you work your dog, keep repeating the commands of COME, DOWN, HEEL, SIT, AND STAY. This will help build his vocabulary and he will more quickly associate the action with the command.

VOICE

- Your voice is an all-important tool in training. It is confusing to a learning dog to coax, wheedle, or sweet-talk him.

- Your voice must have an authoritative ring to it. Your pet must know from your voice that you are in command and will tolerate no foolishness. When he obeys, reward him with praise.

"WAIT"

- When training for obedience competition, you will use the command, "Stay." This means that the dog is to remain in position without moving. However, there are times when you want your dog to stay in a vicinity but don't mind if he moves, such as when you get out of a car. In that case, give the command, "Wait" until you take care of bundles, children, etc.

TRAVEL

There are special problems
With which we come to grips.
How about a check list
Before we start our trips?

AIR TRAVEL

- **Arrival Time**

  - Give recipient of dog the time of arrival, airline, and flight number. Ask to be informed as soon as dog arrives. Dogs do get lost, and the time factor is important in locating your pet.

- **Crates**

  - The crate should be sturdy, leakproof, and just large enough for the pet to stand and move around. Head should touch the top of the crate.

  - Put a familiar pad or rug in the bottom of the cage with a large favorite toy.

  - Print your name, address, phone number, and pet's destination on the crate, indicate if dog will bite. Attach feeding instructions or special instructions.

- **Food and Water**

  - Dry food is best. Put food and dish in a cloth bag attached to the outside of the crate. If canned food must be used, include a can opener.

  - Water dishes attached to the inside of the crate are best as attendants do not have to open the door to give your pet water. Do not leave water in the dish.

- **Health Requirements**

  - A health certificate, indicating rabies and distemper innoculations, is recommended. In some states, this is required.

- **ID**

  - Be sure your dog is wearing proper identification attached to a buckle collar.

- **Jet Flight Conditioning**

  - SEE Conditioning, page 155.

- **Suggestions**

  - If your dog is extremely nervous, ask your veterinarian about a tranquilizer.

  - Do not feed for six hours before the flight.

  - Make sure the dog is exercised before and after the flight.

  - If your dog is riding in a strange crate, leave a familiar rug or toy with him.

  - Straight-through flights are preferable. Check with various airlines.

  - In hot weather, plan the flight so your dog will arrive in the cool of the evening or morning.

  - Certain airlines have better facilities and safety records for live animals.

  - When picking up your dog at the airport, be sure to take a leash and a collar.

CAMPING REGULATIONS

- **Campgrounds**

    - Don't let your pet wander loose. For HIS protection, keep him on leash.

    - Don't leave your dog alone in the camper unless you can be sure he will not get too hot.

    - When provided, use the special area for dogs to relieve themselves. PICK UP YOUR OWN DOG'S DROPPINGS.

- **National Parks and Forests**

    - National Parks generally ban dogs from undeveloped or wilderness areas.

    - In National Forests, dogs may accompany owners on hikes.

    - Most campgrounds and all National Parks require you to keep your pet in a vehicle or tent overnight.

- **Wild Animals**

    - A block of salt from a feed store, placed a distance from your camp, will keep porcupines from getting close and possibly harming your dog. These and other animals are generally looking for a little salt in their diet.

CAR COMFORT

- **Bed**

    - Small dogs can be safely accommodated in a doll bed placed lengthwise behind the front seat. Brackets can be attached and hooked over the front seat at window level so he can see out.

- **Carpet**

  - Indoor-outdoor carpet in the travel crate provides traction and cushioning. It is easy to clean if the dog has an accident. A rubber bath mat serves the same purpose.

- **High Chair**

  - The tiny dog will be happier and enjoy the trip more if a box is placed on the back seat so he can see out. It should be anchored to prevent slipping.

- **Large Dog Bed**

  - A large dog in a small car will be more comfortable if a piece of plywood is fitted over the back seat, extending about two inches behind the front seat. Attach two legs to this extension to reach the floor. Cover with material for traction. Corners should be padded to protect upholstery.

CAR SAFETY

- A crate is the safest method of transporting your dog in a car.

I'd rather ride in the front
So I can look out
But since you make the rules
I'll try not to pout.

- A crate which is too large allows the dog to be tossed about in an accident and may cause injury.

- Glue some non-skid material to the tailgate of your station wagon to prevent slipping when loading your pet.

- Metal barricades between the front and back seat provides some protection for your dog.

- If dog is left free in the car, do not leave the keys in the ignition as the dog may accidentally lock himself in.

- If you do not use a crate or a barricade, place your dog on the floor back of the front seat — or even in the back seat. This gives your dog some protection in case of a sudden stop.

- Lock the car doors when leaving as a child may see "Lassie" and open the door to pet her. If she escapes your "Lassie" may not find her way home.

CAR SICKNESS

- Do not feed or give water four to six hours before a trip.

- Motion-sickness pills available at drug stores are effective. Ask your veterinarian for proper dosage.

- Car sickness is generally a state of mind. Several short, pleasant trips can overcome this problem.

- If your dog acts as though he is going to vomit, indicated by excessive drooling, hold his head UP and make him swallow by rubbing his throat. Do not act concerned or sympathetic or he may later use this act as an attention getter.

  It's getting so I hate
  To start out on a trip.
  I always have to throw up
  And feel like such a drip.

- Sugar will help prevent nausea. Before beginning a trip, give your dog a tablespoon of honey or some candy.

EQUIPMENT

- **Air Freshener**

  - Accidents do happen. After a clean up, it is easier to eliminate the odors with a freshener.

  - Do not use a spray which contains PHENOL or CARBOLIC ACID.

  - SEE Cleaning Products and Sprays, page 13.

- **Blanket**

  - An old blanket, folded, makes an excellent bed for the dog in the car or motel and is easy to launder.

- **Bowl Brush**

  - A long-handled bowl brush makes it easier to clean a soiled crate.

- **Check List**

  - Prepare a permanent check list of vital equipment needed for traveling with your dog. Attach to the crate, door of van, or wherever handy. This eliminates confusion and problems.

  There's a list of essentials
  As we start out on our trip...
  Check them over carefully and
  Then let's let 'er rip.

- SEE Sample Check List in APPENDIX.

- **Clean-Up**

  - To pick up after your pet, take a pooper-scooper or small shovel and stick and a supply of plastic bags.

- **Collars and Tags**

  - The dog's personal ID, rabies, and license tags should be attached to a buckle collar and worn at all times.

- **Crates**

  - The best and safest idea when traveling is to put your dog in a crate. It will keep him from skidding around in an accident. He will be unable to run away if the door is left open or there is an accident. He'll be better taken care of and can be transported easier if something happens to you. This is important if your dog isn't friendly.

- Mesh wire crates are ideal for station wagons and vans. You don't have to worry about ventilation; dogs are visible, and crates fold up for compact storage.

- Fiberglass crates are preferred for an open vehicle or pickup truck as they provide shelter from wind and rain.

- **Emergency Travel Kit**

Activated Charcoal	Clorox	Pepto-Bismol Tablets
Adhesive Tape, 1''	Cotton Swabs	Scissors, Blunt
Ammonia, Spirits of	Gauze, 2''	Surgical Soap
Antihistamine Tablets	Hot Water Bottle	Thermometer
(Prescription)	Hydrogen Peroxide	Tomato Juice
Anti-Venom Kit	Kaopectate	(Dehydrated)
Baking Soda	Motion Sickness Tablets	Tweezers
Boric Acid	(Prescription)	Vinegar

- **Flea Powder**

  - This is a must if you wish to avoid fleas on your travels.

- **Health Certificate**

  - Some states, Mexico, and Canada require health certificates. Check with your veterinarian before starting on a trip.

- **Mosquito Repellent**

  - Heartworm is caused by the bite of a certain mosquito. If traveling in an endemic area, carry repellent with you.

- **Paper Products**

  - Paper towels and toilet tissue make cleanups much easier.

  - A small stack of newspapers may come in handy.

  - Take a supply of plastic bags — large and small.

  - A box of facial tissue is a "must" for both you and your dog.

- **Rope**

  - A 15-foot rope or line will have many uses.

- **Shoe Bag**

  - A shoe bag, divided into approximately ten compartments, is ideal to hold small, often misplaced articles, such as, rags, leashes, extra shoes, plastic bags, etc. This bag can be hung on a wall or door of a van or over the back seat of your car.

FOOD AND WATER

- **Food**

  - Try not to feed your dog for six hours before traveling.

  - Your pet's own bowl will give him a sense of security.

  - Dry or canned food is ideal for traveling.

  - Don't feed immediately at destination...wait for one or two hours.

- **Water**

  - Water is a frequent cause of digestive upsets. Start out with a container of water from home and replenish with local water as used...thus providing a gradual change-over.

    We'll surely need water
    To quench our thirst.
    Let's take some from home
    And use it first.

  - A gallon plastic jug filled almost to the top with water and frozen will provide cool drinking water for you and your dog. If placed in an ice chest, it will also keep other food cool and fresh.

  - A dash of lemon, added to strange drinking water, will help to prevent digestive upsets. It will also discourage too much intake of water. This helps to eliminate frequent rest stops.

- A water dish attached to the crate, filled with ice cubes, will provide cool water.

- To have fresh water available without spills, purchase a pet waterer (pet supply store) which is a glass or plastic bottle with a ball point tube and holder. Fasten to the crate at a comfortable height.

- Glucose added to the water will discourage the pangs of hunger.

FOREIGN TRAVEL

- Inquire well in advance for the regulations of each foreign country you will visit. Your veterinarian may be able to supply this information. If not, check with a foreign consulate.

- Most countries require a health certificate and proof of rabies vaccination.

- Some countries have a quarantine period for the dog before he can enter that country.

HAZARDS

- **Choke Collar**

    - NEVER leave a choke collar (training collar) on a crated dog or one loose in the car. It might catch on something and the dog, in his efforts to free himself, may strangle.

        Training collars
          Have only one use.
        As permanent things
          They can only abuse.

- **Dognapping**

    - Be sure dog is locked in the car.

    - An alarm system can be installed in the car.

    - If possible, park the car where the dog is visible.

- Avoid bumper stickers telling the world you have a valuable show dog in your car or trailer.

- **Heads Protruding from Auto**

  - Dogs with heads out of an open window are inviting eye and ear infection, even serious head injury.

- **Heartworm**

  - Heartworm is extremely serious. If traveling in an endemic area, ask your veterinarian about a prophylactic (preventive) medicine.

- **Pickup Trucks**

  - NEVER put your dog in the bed of a pickup truck. A sudden stop could throw him in the path of a car. You are legally responsible if there is an accident because of your negligence.

    Do you see the loose dogs
    In the back of that truck?
    If they should fall out
    They'd surely be struck.

HOT WEATHER

- **Carpet**

  - In extremely hot weather, the carpet in the crate can be wet down and the dampness and evaporation will help to keep the dog cooler. Replace with a dry carpet at night.

- **Coolers**

  - A bucket or plastic tub filled with ice and placed in the rear of the station wagon helps keep the car cooler.

- **Dark Dogs**

  - Dark or black dogs are more susceptible to heat than other colors so extra care must be taken to protect them from the heat.

- **Feeding**

  - Feed your dog lightly and give fresh water frequently.

- **In Cars**

  - A parked car with the air conditioning left on is dangerous as the motor may stall, turning the cool air into an oven.

  - A tightly closed car parked in the sun IS A DEATH TRAP, especially in the summer. Allow for cross ventilation, park in the shade, and check the dog frequently.

- **Spray Bottle**

  - A squirt of water in the dog's mouth will relieve thirst.

  - In hot weather, if a dog must be kept in the car, spray his coat well with cool water. A couple of ice cubes in the bottle will keep the water cool.

- **Sun Shades**

  - Sun screens and other types of blinds on the INSIDE of the car windows are of little help as the heat has already penetrated the glass.

  - A light-colored car is cooler than a dark one.

  - Pittsburg Plate Glass Company has a product called Aluminized Mylar which can be taped on the outside of the glass and makes an excellent reflective surface.

  - If buying a new car, order windows that have a vapor-deposited metallic coating that will reflect sunlight.

- **Wet Towels**

    - If it is very hot in the car, a wet towel over the wire crate will cause evaporation and keep your dog cooler.

HOTELS

- A directory of hotels and motels that accommodate guests with dogs (TOURING WITH TOWSER) may be obtained from the Gaines TWT, P.O. Box 1007, Kankakee, IL 60901.

- The American Automobile Association (AAA) provides a list of hotels and motels that will accept dogs.

- Many motels will allow dogs if they are crated so as not to cause any damage.

- When you leave a dog crated in a motel room, attach a note to his crate saying where you may be contacted in case of an emergency. NEVER leave a barker unattended.

- Leave a tip and note to the maid thanking her for any inconvenience you might have caused.

- When you check out, make a point of thanking the management for the privilege of keeping your dog with you.

- Inquire where you may exercise your dog and stay within that area. Do not allow your dog to damage bushes and flowers. Keep walks clean by curbing your dog. Pick up stools.

- If damage is done, tell the management and willingly pay for the damage.

- Do not bathe your dog in the tub or use hotel linen to dry him.

- If dog is not crated, tie him so he will not escape when maid comes into the room to clean.

- When walking your dog keep him on a leash.

- When out of the room, keep your dog in a crate to prevent chewing and soiling.

STANDARD OPERATING PROCEDURE

- **Do**

  - Before any trip or short jaunt, allow your dog to relieve himself.

  - Put your dog on a six-foot lead or long rope. Find a good spot then stand and let him circle you until he relieves himself. This method takes less time than if he investigates the entire area first.

  - You will find that much time can be saved if you have trained your dog to go "on command." SEE Housebreaking on Signal, page 163.

  - Assign a special spot in the car for your dog; then insist he stay there. Provide an old blanket or pad for his exclusive use.

  - Teach your dog to mind his own business when you are driving.

  - Train your dog to stay in the car when you open the door. When you release him from the command, praise profusely.

  - Your dog should have all required shots before you start on a trip. Most states require a health certificate which must be completed by your veterinarian. Keep all records with you.

- If your dog is used to wearing a sweater, take one along even if the weather is warm. The temperature could change.

- After exercising your dog in a public area where there have been many dogs, it would be wise to dip his feet in a clorox or salt solution before loading him back in the car.

- If your dog is not a seasoned traveler, it might be well to ask your veterinarian for a mild tranquilizer to use the first couple of days of the trip. It could even come in handy in case there is an emergency.

- Take your dog out of the car on a leash — no matter how well trained he is. A dog lost in an unfamiliar area is often hard to find.

- Provide an old suitcase for just your dog. Pack it with his dishes, cans of food, can opener, sweater, medication, first aid kit, chew bones, toys, long line for exercising, and treats. Everything he needs will be in one spot and your automobile will not be so cluttered.

- **Don'ts**
  - Never put a dog in the trunk of a car with the lid up or down, crated or uncrated. It could be cold and drafty but the greatest danger is the possibility of carbon monoxide poisoning.

  - A golden rule of the road is not to do anything away from home that you and your dog wouldn't do at home.

  - Never fasten a leash to the steering wheel when you leave the car. If the dog should jump over the seat, he could be in trouble.

  - Do not let your dog bark or become uncontrollable when he sees other dogs or people. It is dangerous and annoying.

  - Do NOT LEAVE a dog in the car without proper care being given to ventilation and shade.

  - Do not allow dog to ride with head out of the window.

MISCELLANEOUS

These pages are miscellaneous
  As you can see.
They don't fit any one category,
  Just like me.

ALLERGIES

- A person who is allergic to dogs may not be allergic to cats and vice versa.

- Some experts believe that people allergic to dogs find breeds that do not shed (like poodles) are less troublesome. Most allergists agree, however, that if a person is allergic to one dog, he's allergic to all.

ALLERGY TO DRUGS

- If your dog is highly allergic to certain drugs, indicate this information on his I.D. collar. If he becomes lost medical attention can be given to him.

ANESTHETICS

- If you bring your dog home after an operation before the anesthesia has worn off, don't be alarmed if he snaps, has "running" dreams, appears groggy and uncoordinated. Put him in a dark room and don't feed for at least 12 hours.

BAKING SODA

- Is great for freshening and cleaning up small areas in the kennel.

Your great grandma used soda
  To bake and to scour.
S'pose she knew it can keep
  Our runs from turning sour?

- Is ideal when used to eliminate odors from upholstered furniture. Apply and allow to remain one hour before vacuuming.

BITCHES IN HEAT

- Chlorophyll tablets to mask heat odors of females may be purchased from a pet supply store or veterinarian.

- The best protection from visiting males is to confine your bitch.

- Transport your bitch in the car to an area away from your home to answer nature's call.

- Wash the vulva area frequently with products which contain chlorophyll. May be purchased at pet supply stores.

- Britches for your bitch may be purchased. They protect furniture, carpet, etc., from stains and odors.

- Do not depend upon any product to discourage males during the last ten days of a cycle.

CANINE FRIENDS

- Two dogs are not much more care than one. They play together and are more mentally alert. By entertaining one another, they relieve you of the responsibility. Ideally they should be of opposite sex and approximately the same age and size.

COLLARS

- Buckle collars are made of leather or cotton webbing. Size of collar should be the neck's circumference, plus three inches.

- Nylon collars, either woven or stitched, are strong and will not harm the coat. However, there is a slower response time in training.

- Metal choke collars come in a variety of shapes and weights. The chain slips through the ring more smoothly if there are more links. Should not have rough edges that can cut. Inexpensive chain collars may rust or discolor the coat. For strength buy a "butt weld" where no bump is evident.

DOG'S BODY LANGUAGE

- "Let's Play"

  - Tail wags and is held high
  - Bows, hindquarters higher than shoulders
  - Ears forward
  - Prances
  - Barks

- "I Love You"

  - Licking with a straight tongue

- "I Surrender" (submissive)

  - Dog avoids eye contact
  - Ears flattened against head
  - Tail low, slow wag
  - Some dogs roll over on back
  - Some crawl on their stomach
  - Others may wet the floor

- "Your Presence Disturbs Me" (fear bitter)

  - Ears flat against head
  - Hackles up
  - Tail tucked between legs
  - Weight shifted to rear
  - May attack if approached

- "No Holds Barred" (attack)

  - Head held high
  - Ears forward
  - Direct stare
  - Lips pulled back
  - Tongue curled back toward nose
  - Hackles raised
  - Snarling - barking - growling
  - Slow wag of stand-up tail

DOG SITTER'S DILEMMA

- For three days the lonesome dog refused to eat. The dog sitter hired by the vacationing family was desperate. She noticed the dog always sniffed her, then turned away. So as a last resort the sitter put on the lady's long robe. The dog sniffed it, his tail wagged, and the hunger strike was broken.

DOORS

- Tired of letting your dog in and out of the house? Install a pet door which permits ingress and egress from house to yard. Information may be obtained in pet magazines or at local pet supply stores.

DROOLING

- Excessive salivation may be caused by hunger, enticing smells, excitement, or fear. However, it is wise to check the mouth for a bad tooth or sore.

- Poisonous plants or substances may also cause drooling.

- For some dogs drooling is normal. The St. Bernards, for example, drool excessively due to the formation of their lips.

ESTRUS — HEAT CYCLES

- First Estrus   —   6-12 months

- Sign   —   Bloody vaginal discharge

- Length   —   3-4 weeks

- Frequency   —   Usually every six months

- Cycling   —   Entire life

FECES

- If your dog appears ill, observe his feces and report to the veterinarian. It can be important for a diagnosis.

- The stool should be firm, not fluid.

- Blood in the stool may be caused by the irritation of a foreign object or even irritating food. If condition persists, see a veterinarian.

- Black, tarry stools indicate blood in the small intestine. This could be serious.

- Mucous and slimy stools signify an inflamed colon, irritating foods, or whipworm.

- White to light tan feces indicates a problem with the pancreas.

- Gray stools indicate insufficient bile is being secreted by the liver.

- Hard, pellet-shaped stools indicate constipation caused by incorrect feeding, eating bones, lack of exercise, or enlargement of the prostate gland. If this problem is not corrected, peritonitis could result.

FLY CONTROL

- Sticky fly paper in the kennel area is a safe and effective device to reduce the fly population.

GROOMING

- If you wish to clip and groom your dog according to AKC Standard for your breed, check the public library for books on grooming.

- SEE Chapter on Grooming, page 69.

HAIR ANALYSIS

- Analysis of hair is fairly new in the medical field but is being used more and more by veterinarians. The readings from the hair sample tell the veterinarian of any mineral imbalance. It also shows the presence of toxic metals which may be corrected by preventive medicine and nutrition.

HAIR RECYCLING

- Hair collected from grooming, if planted around flowers and shrubs, will improve plants. This is due to the protein in the hair.

- After brushing your long-haired dog, don't throw away the hair. Collect it and when you think you have enough you can have it spun by a professional spinner. The yarn can be made into sweaters, scarves, gloves, etc.

HAIR IN REFRIGERATOR MOTOR

- If your long-haired dog has the run of the house, be sure to clean the motor area of the refrigerator regularly. Dirt, dust, and dog hair can cause serious mechanical problems.

HAIR REMOVERS

- Buy a pair of textured rubber gloves, dampen them, and rub over your clothing. Like magic, the hair adheres to the gloves.

- Slightly dampen a sponge and rub over the material to remove hair from furniture, clothes, or car.

- Sticky tape wound around your hand helps to pick up loose hair on clothing and furniture.

HEARING-EAR DOGS

- Dogs are now being trained to aid deaf people. They alert their owners to sounds such as alarm clocks, door bells, knocking, smoke alarms, etc. This gives the deaf person the same sense of security that seeing-eye dogs give to the blind.

- Check with your veterinarian or librarian for experts trained in this field.

HOME VS HOSPITAL CARE

- Unless your dog has been badly injured or needs to be kept under the watchful eye of a veterinarian, it is better to nurse your dog at home. Separation from those he loves and unfamiliar surroundings may aggravate his condition. TLC IS VERY IMPORTANT!

- It is invaluable to the veterinarian if you keep a record of the nursing care you give your dog.

- SEE Appendix, Chart on Home Care.

ICE—SNOW—FROSTBITE

- Before letting your dogs out to romp in the snow, apply petroleum vaseline generously between the toes of each foot. This will prevent the formation of ice balls which can cause a great deal of discomfort.

- Frostbite is indicated by the skin or pads turning gray to white, swelling, and soreness. It may lead eventually to infection and gangrene.

- Treatment of frostbite is to warm the area by applying warm (not hot) moist towels frequently. It may be necessary to give antibiotics to prevent infection.

INSURANCE

- Some companies issue policies for dog owners which will cover hospitalization, death, etc. There are policies that even cover damage to hotel rooms. Insurance policies are expensive but may be worth it.

- Check your home owner's policy to see if you are covered in case your dog bites someone or destroys property.

LACTATING BITCHES

- Give one tablespoon of bee pollen per 50 pounds of body weight, daily.

- If the bitch doesn't have enough milk, give her a few swallows of beer. This usually brings on milk in abundant quantities. The small amount of alcohol will not affect the puppies.

- A nursing bitch requires three to four balanced feedings a day. Diet should include a good grade of dog food, cottage cheese, meat, or cooked eggs. Give plenty of liquid.

- Instead of giving the bitch powdered or canned milk, use one of the milk replacers on the market for calves.

LAST WILL AND TESTAMENT

- What will happen to your dog if you and your immediate family are killed? Your beloved pet may suffer if you haven't made arrangements for him. Many relatives can't or won't assume the responsibility. It would be better if you contact friends or breeders now to find someone willing to adopt him. If your dog isn't tatooed, write a description and attach a photograph. Include this with his papers, health record, etc. This procedure is very important if you have several dogs of the same breed.

If anything dreadful
  Should happen to you
What in the world
  Would I ever do!

LAW AND THE DOG

- States and communities differ regarding the many liabilities, responsibilities, and rights for you as a dog owner. If you are unable to answer all of the following questions, check with local authorities.

  1. Are dog licenses required?

  2. Is there a leash law?

3. How many dogs am I allowed?

4. Is there a law about dogs that bark excessively?

5. What if my dog destroys personal property of others?

6. Could I be arrested if I take in a stray dog?

7. Is it a misdemeanor if my dog befouls a sidewalk or public area?

8. If I injure a dog with a car, what are my responsibilities?

9. What is the lawful procedure to be followed if my dog bites someone?

10. Am I legally responsible if my dog causes a car accident?

• These are only a few of the possible laws pertaining to you and your dog. Be knowledgeable of your responsibilities.

LEASHES

• An inexpensive leash can be made from a plastic water-ski rope. Purchase a snap fastener and tape on one end.

LIFE JACKETS

• Many boat owners who take their pets aboard are apprehensive for their safety. A dog can swim, but he can also drown, depending on the water conditions, the time in the water, and possible fright. Life jackets for dogs are made by TEXAS WATER CRAFTERS CO., Wichita Falls, Texas.

LIMPING

• Check pads of the feet for thorns, cuts, or matted hair.

- Should your dog develop a lameness in the hindquarters, confine him. If, after three days, the lameness continues, take the dog to the veterinarian. Do not allow medication to mask the pain for if it is a ligament tear, the condition will worsen. An operation may be indicated.

LITTER IDENTIFICATION FOR NEW-BORN PUPPIES

- Have as many different colored grosgrain ribbons as there are puppies. The ribbon should be narrow and tied in a knot with the ends cut short.

This mother love within me
Is tender and it's deep.
How many of these tykes
Do you plan to let me keep?

- It takes time for Mercurochrome to wear away, so dab according to your prearranged code. It is a quick and easy method of identification.

- If you have several litters all about the same age, take scissors and clip a small area of hair right down to the skin on one leg, for example, the right leg. For litter number two, clip the left leg, etc. Be sure to record these marking codes.

MOLE REPELLENT

- Dog hair from combing and clipping, if stuffed into a mole hole, will discourage the little critters.

- If moles are raising havoc in your yard, place a scoop of dog stools in the mole holes. The neighbors will hate you when the moles move next door.

OBLITERATING ODORS

- Vita-Aire machines, which combine negative ions with impurities in the air and destroy them through oxidation, come in many different models. Operation costs are negligible. This process is effective in destroying airborne bacteria and dust.

- Dog odor in furniture can be eliminated by sprinkling baking soda on the material, let stand for an hour, and then vacuum.

PARVOVIRUS DISINFECTANT

- The only known effective disinfectant at this time for the dreaded parvovirus is a water and a Clorox solution (30-1). Keep your premises disinfected. After walking your dog in a public area, dip his feet in this solution and clean the soles of your own shoes.

RECORDED VOICE

- A dog will not be so upset when left alone if you record your voice on a tape and play it during your absence.

RESPONSIBILITIES OF DOG OWNERS

- Keep your dog confined on your own property.

- Correct and train a barking dog.

- Do not build kennel runs too close to your neighbor's property.

- Pick up stools frequently.

- Do not allow your dog to jump on visitors.

- If your dog is sick, do not expose to other dogs.

- Always pick up stools as you walk your dog.

SKUNKS

- Tomato juice is excellent to deodorize skunk odors. Dehydrated tomato juice takes very little room and can be carried easily by campers.

Seeing that black and white kitty
  I just wanted to play.
Nobody ever told me about
  The horrible stuff he can spray.

SNIFFING

- Do not allow your dog to sniff hydrants, posts, trees, etc. Diseases may be transmitted this way.

SPAYING

- Spaying is a form of birth control in which the bitch's ovaries are surgically removed.

- The disadvantages of spaying are only two. The female is ineligible to compete in AKC dog shows (but may compete in obedience trials), and she will be unable to have puppies.

- The advantages are too numerous but a few are no more messy heat periods, no unwanted and unloved puppies, no uninvited males, fewer breast tumors, less likelihood of pyometra (serious urine infection), and licenses will cost less. Most important advantage is that spaying will prevent millions of unwanted dogs from being destroyed each year.

STROKING

- It is better to stroke a dog instead of patting. Stroking is soothing, patting can make some dogs nervous.

TAILS

- Hunting dogs often acquire a sore tip on the tail from briars and underbrush. Cut a finger from an old leather glove, slip over the tip of the tail, and fasten with adhesive tape.

TEETH

- Puppies have 28 baby teeth; as an adult they will have 42 permanent teeth. Baby teeth will fall out at about three months of age and be replaced with permanent teeth by six months.

TIMID DOGS

- The timid dog needs more exposure to people and noise. However, do this gradually. It is helpful to take short trips to shopping centers, along busy streets, or by school playgrounds at recess.

I don't want to be a coward
And always run and hide.
But my life has been so protected
With you always by my side.

- Rough and tumble play and kind treatment make the timid dog more outgoing.

- Many timid dogs have responded well to obedience training due to their association with other dogs and people.

TONSILLITIS

- Infected tonsils can be painful and debilitating to your dog. Symptoms are lacks appetite, has very little energy, coughs, gags, vomits, paws at base of ear, and has a swelling just below the jaws. See your veterinarian.

UNDESIRABLE MATING OR ABORTION

- An abortion can be accomplished by hormone injections. The time period should be between the eighth and tenth day.

VISITS TO VETERINARIAN

- Call for an appointment.

- If there is an emergency, have someone call ahead and give nature of the problem so equipment can be made ready.

- Make a list of questions to ask the veterinarian.

- Dog should always be on a leash.

- Sit as far as possible from other owners and dogs.

- Keep large dogs in down position at your feet.

- Discourage small children from petting "Lassie."

- A treat given to your dog before and after a visit to the veterinarian may alleviate some of his reluctance and fear.

WADING POOL

- Like children, dogs love to splash in water, especially on hot summer days. A child's wading pool set up in the shade provides entertainment and helps to keep the dog cool.

WHELPING SANITATION

- Keep excess hair out of the way for whelping by cutting off an old pair of panty hose and slipping on the bitch. Put a hole in the appropriate place. This also works for breeding.

Seems like yesterday
   When I was your baby.
Now all at once, here I am
   A very pregnant lady.

- Most breeders will shave down a long-haired bitch about to give whelp. They usually shave off the britches and the upper tail. The coat will eventually be shed anyway and shaving makes sanitation easier and minimizes the chance of infection.

- The tail of a collie or other breeds with long plumy tails can be protected during whelping by slipping a long stocking around the tail and wrapping with adhesive tape.

WHISTLE

- If you call your dog by means of a whistle, you will not annoy your neighbors if you use a silent or Galton Whistle.

Finis, finale
This has to be the end.
Now, you'll have more time
For your ever-loving friend.

VITAL INFORMATION

VETERINARIAN_____

    Address_____ Phone No._____

EMERGENCY CLINIC_____

    Address_____ Phone No._____

POISON-CONTROL CENTER_____

    Address_____ Phone No._____

ANIMAL CONTROL CENTER_____

    Address_____ Phone No._____

HUMANE SOCIETY/S.P.C.A._____

    Address_____ Phone No._____

FRIEND/NEIGHBOR/BABY-SITTER_____

    Address_____ Phone No._____

PET SUPPLY STORE_____

    Address_____ Phone No._____

_____

DOG'S BIRTH DATE_____   TATOO IDENTIFICATION

REGISTRATION NO._____   NO._____

LICENSE NO._____   RABIES TAG NO._____

MEDICAL RECORD

NAME_____ BIRTH DATE_____ BREED_____

IMMUNIZATION RECORD

DISEASE & BOOSTERS	DATE
DISTEMPER_____	
HEPATITIS_____	
LEPTOSPIROSIS_____	
PARVOVIRUS_____	
RABIES_____	

WORMING — TYPE

SURGERY

ILLNESSES

SENSITIVITIES & UNUSUAL REACTIONS:

HOME NURSING CHART

	A.M.	P.M.
FOOD (Amount and Kind)		
MEDICATION (Kind)		
MEDICATION (Time Given)		
STOOLS		
TEMPERATURE		
URINE		
VOMITING		
WATER (Amount)		
UNUSUAL SIGNS		

NAMES—FEMALE

Colors		Characteristics	
ADRIENNE	Dark	ADA	Happy
ALBINA	White	ADINA	Gentle
AMBER	Yellow	AGATHA	Good
AURELIA	Golden	ALLEGRA	Lively
BIANCA	White	ATHENA	Wise
BRENNA	Black	AUDREY	Strong
CANDACE	White	BENA	Wise
DARCIE	Dark	BRINA	Protectress
DARENE	Golden	CARA	Friend
DEIDRE	Black	CARLA	Strong
ELECTRA	Amber	CHARLOTTE	Strong
FLAVIA	Yellow	CLEO	Famed
GUINEVERE	White	DULCIE	Sweet
GWENDOLYN	White	FELICIA	Happy
GWYNETH	White	FIDELIA	Faithful
LEILA	Dark	HAIDEE	Bashful
MELANIE	Dark	HAILA	Strong
ORLENA	Golden	HILARY	Merry
RUBY	Red	IDA	Happy
ROWENA	White	INGRID	Beautiful
		IRMA	Strong
MS		JACINDA	Comely
		JOCELYN	Fair
COLLEEN	Girl	JOLI	Pretty
CORA	Maiden	LETITIA	Joyful
DIOSA	Goddess	LOLA	Strong
DONNA	Lady	MEGAN	Strong
DORENE	Golden Girl	MIGNON	Dainty
GRISELDA	Heroine	MINERVA	Wise
KOREN	Young Girl	NARDA	Joyous
LASSIE	Girl	OLA	Protectress
LEDY	Lady	PAULA	Little
LOIS	Battle Maiden	RAGGIL	Rascal
NATALIE	Christmas Child	REGINA	Queenlike
PATRICIA	Noble Lady	SERENA	Quiet
REGINA	Queen	WANDA	Wanderer
SABRINA	Princess	WILDA	Wild One
TANIA	Fairy Queen	YOLANDA	Shy

NAMES — MALE

Colors		Characteristics	
ADRIAN	Black	ALAN	Handsome
ALBAN	White	ALGERNON	With whiskers
BOYD	Yellow	ALVIN	Friend to all
BRUNO	Brown	ARGUS	Watchful
DEWITT	White	BERNARD	Bold
DOUGAL	Black	BORIS	Fighter
DOUGLAS	Gray	BRICE	Alert
DUNCAN	Brown	CALVIN	Bald
GRIFFITH	Red	CAMERON	Crooked nose
GWYNNE	White	CECIL	Blind
KENYON	Yellow	CLAUDE	Lame
LLOYD	Gray	CONAN	Wise
MAURICE	Dark	CONRAD	Brave
MORGAN	White	COURTNEY	Short nose
MURRAY	Red	CRISPIN	Curly haired
NIGEL	Black	DALLAS	Spirited
RORY	Red	DILLON	Faithful
RUFUS	Red	ENOCH	Devoted
RUSSEL	Red	ESAU	Hairy
SHERLOCK	Yellow	ETHAN	Steadfast
		EZRA	Helper

MR

ALARIC	Ruler	FERGUS	Strong
		GALE	Lively
ANDREW	Manly	GREGORY	Vigilant
BORIS	Fighter	GUNTHER	Bold
BRIAN	Leader	HILARY	Happy
CHANNING	King	JAY	Lively
CHARLES	Manly	JULIUS	Soft-haired
DONALD	Ruler	KEVIN	Comely
DUSTIN	Fighter	KYLE	Handsome
ERIC	Kingly	LANG	Tall
KIM	Chief	OTIS	Keen-eared
MAGNUS	Great	ORSON	Bear-like
REGAN	King	PAUL	Little
REX	King	SHERWIN	True friend
VICTOR	Conqueror	TRISTRAM	Sad faced
WARRICK	Ruler	VAUGHN	Small
		WYATT	Guide

DOG-SITTER'S INSTRUCTION SHEET

EXERCISE	
FOOD & TIME	
MEDICATION	
WATER	

PHONE NUMBERS

Owner's_____   Emergency Clinic_____

Friend/Neighbor_____   Poison Control_____

Veterinarian_____

OTHER INSTRUCTIONS

TRAVEL CHECK-OFF LIST

ITEMS	TRIPS								
	1	2	3	4	5	6	7	8	9
Bedding									
Collar									
Crate									
Deodorant Spray									
Dishes									
First Aid Kit									
Flea Spray									
Food									
Health Certificate									
I.D. Tag									
Leash & Rope									
Medication									
Mosquito Spray									
Newspapers									
Paper Towels									
Plastic Bags									
Pooper Scooper									
Rabies Certificate									
Towels									
Water									

VITAMINS — MINERALS

VITAMIN	FUNCTION	SOURCE
A (Carotene) Fat Soluble	Prevents dryness of skin and dry coat. Promotes tissue formation. Essential to health of eyes. Benefits bone growth.	Butter, cheese, carrots, dandelion greens, egg yolk, green leafy vegetables, milk, liver, seafood.
B-1 (Thiamine)	Improves appetite. Builds blood. Promotes growth and energy. Relieves pain. Essential to pregnant bitches. Strengthens muscles.	Bran, cereal, brewer's yeast, wheat germ, kelp, dandelion greens, parsley, pork, beef.
B-2 (Riboflavin)	Effectual in skin diseases. Makes dog less susceptible to infectious diseases, improves muscles.	Animal organs, beet tops, brewer's yeast, cheese, eggs, bran, dried milk, spinach, kelp.
B-3 (Niacin)	Improves skin and coat. Aids in digestion. Helps correct black tongue.	Beef, brewer's yeast, fish, brown rice, chicken, hearts, liver, turkey, wheat bran.
B-6 (Pyridoxine)	Helps muscles and nerves. Aids in skin disease. Effective in epilepsy and anemia. Relieves spastic paralysis of hindquarters.	Alfalfa, beef, beef heart and liver, chicken, molasses, wheat germ, brewer's yeast, dried peas.
B-12 (Cobalamin)	Treatment for anemia. Helps respiratory problems. Aids in hives, rashes and some skin problems.	Cheese, egg yolk, and liver.
C (Ascorbic Acid) Water Soluble	Aids in infection. Helps with respiratory problems. Effective in healing. Aids teeth and gums.	Green leafy vegetables, green peppers, liver, milk, parsley, sproated grains, tomatoes.
D Fat Soluble	Aids in mending and strengthening bones. Effective in skin health. Regulates calcium and phosphorus in the blood. Effectual treatment of rickets.	Butter, cod liver oil, egg yolk, fish, milk, sunlight.

VITAMINS

VITAMIN	FUNCTION	SOURCE
E (Tocopherol) Fat Soluble	Aids in sterility. Restores healthy hair. Formation of new skin (from burns, etc.) Helps in arthritis.	Milk, wheat germ, whole grain cereal, vegetable oil.
F	Promotes growth. Improves skin and coat health.	Cod liver oil, milk, safflower oil, soybean oil, sunflower oil.

MINERALS

MINERAL	FUNCTION	SOURCE
Calcium	Necessary for bones and teeth. Prevents skin problems. Helps in clotting of blood. Nerve health.	Bone meal, buttermilk, milk, cheese, dandelion greens, parsley, yogurt.
Iron	Produces hemoglobin, improves endurance. Aids in anemia. Transports oxygen in blood. Aids in hookworm infestation.	Blackstrap molasses, parsley, dandelion greens, egg yolk, liver, wheat germ.
Magnesium	Important to reproduction and growth. Helps in function of calcium and phosphorus. Formation of bone and teeth.	Bran, dandelion greens, honey, kelp, spinach.
Iodine	Regulates metabolism. Important to thyroid health and normal growth. Aids in sterility. Helps in skin diseases.	Foods grown in iodine-rich soil, fish and shell fish.
Potassium	Aids in growth. Aids blood-shot and watery eyes. Lack causes gas formation.	Blackstrap molasses, potatoes, tomatoes. (One teaspoon honey and natural undistilled cider vinegar.)

PEDIGREE

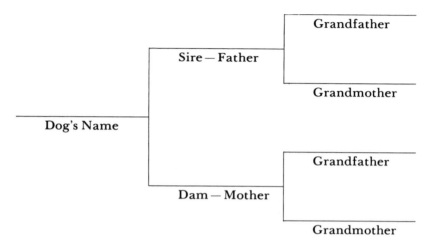

		Grandfather
Sire — Father		
		Grandmother

Dog's Name

		Grandfather
Dam — Mother		
		Grandmother

Registered Name   Call Name

Birth Date   Breed

Breeder   Address

Purchased by   Date

> *My master explained*
> *Because of my family tree*
> *Only a blue blood*
> *Is good enough for me.*

SOURCES OF INFORMATION

ORGANIZATIONS

AMERICAN DOG OWNERS ASS'N.
P.O. Box 746
Albany, NY   12207

THE AMERICAN KENNEL CLUB
51 Madison Avenue
New York, NY   10010

THE CANADIAN KENNEL CLUB
2150 Bloor Street West
Toronto, Ontario   M6S 4V7

MIXED BREED DOG CLUBS OF AMERICA
Box 281
Redmond, WA   98052

MAGAZINES

ANIMALS
350 S. Huntington Avenue
Boston, MA   02130
(Magazine of Am. Humane Society)

DOG FANCY MAGAZINE
P.O. Box 2430
Boulder, CO   80321

DOG GROOMERS GAZETTE
616 E. Manhatton Drive
Tempe, AZ   85282

DOG WORLD
32 New Street
Ashford, Kent, England   TN24 8UX

DOG WORLD MAGAZINE
300 West Adams Street
Chicago, IL   60606

DOGS
251 Park Avenue South
New York, NY   10010

DOGS OF CANADA
3 Church Street
Toronto, Ontario, Canada   M5E IM2

FRONT AND FINISH
P.O. Box 333

Galesburg, IL   61401
(Newsletter for Dog Trainers)

KENNEL REVIEW
828 N. LaBrea Avenue
Hollywood, CA   90038

NATIONAL DOG
P.O. Box 399
Lomita, CA   90717

OFF LEAD
P.O. Box 307
Graves Road
Westmoreland, NY   13490
(Dog Training Magazine)

OFFICIAL DOGS
257 Park Avenue South
New York, NY   10010

PURE BRED DOGS
American Kennel Gazette
51 Madison Avenue
New York, NY   10010

TODAY'S DOG
2470 Lemoine Avenue
Fort Lee, NJ   07024

TERMS USED BY DOG FANCIERS

AKC	American Kennel Club
Apron	Long hair on dog's chest — frill
Bitch	Female dog
Blaze	White streak down the middle of head
Blooded	Pedigreed dog
Breeder	Owner of a bitch at time of whelping
Broken color	Self color broken by another color
Burr	The inside of the ear
Canines	Two upper and two lower fang-like teeth
Castrate	To remove testicles
Cow-hocked	Inward turning of hocks
Condition	General health, coat and appearance
Cropping	Cutting dog's ears to make them stand erect and pointing
Crossbreed	To breed between two varieties of the same species
Cryptorchid	Male with neither testicle descended
Dam	A female parent
Dew claw	Extra toe occasionally present on inside of leg
Docking	Cutting or shortening the tail
Dog	Male dog — used collectively for males and females
Fall	Hair overhanging the face
Feathering	Longer hair on ears, legs, tail
Haw	An inner eyelid — third eyelid
Heat	Estrum — seasonal period of the bitch
Hip Dysplasia	A genetic disorder of the hip joint
Inbreeding	Mating of closely related dogs
Leather	Skin of the ears
Litter	Puppies of one whelping
Mane	Thick hair on the neck
Mask	Dark shading on muzzle of some dogs
Pad	Sole of feet
Pastern	Leg below the knee
Pedigree	Written record of dog's lineage
Pricked ears	Naturally erect ears
Registration	Before being exhibited, dogs must be registered with AKC
Ruff	Thick and longer hair around the neck
Sire	Male parent
Spayed	Female whose ovaries have been surgically removed
Stud dog	Male dog used for breeding
Undershot	Lower teeth projecting above the uppers
Withers	Highest point of the shoulders

INDEX

INDEX

INDEX

INDEX

INDEX

INDEX

INDEX

INDEX

Design by: Roz Pape   Printed by: Murray Publishing Company, Seattle, Washington